HIDING
IN
PLAIN SIGHT

A TESTIMONY FOR LIVING

THERESA MILES

Book design by www.delaney-designs.com

ISBN: 978-1-09839-047-1

PREFACE

Perhaps an odd title, I suppose, but it will become clearer as you read on. The realities of my past will give you a better understanding of one path of rediscovery... long over-shadowed by other's expectations. This is a testament of my personal challenge to live my authentic life vs. how others expect how that life should be lived. I want to share something for you to use and hopefully avoid those pitfalls, realizing that everyone is different, but that we are more alike than you may think.

Writing this testament gives me some 'self-therapy' by probing my past to help resurface some pain-points that have been left dormant... to dust them off and deal with them. To put all things into perspective. Like many, there are elements of my past I never want to repeat. But I also know that I would never trade them—for they've molded my character and helped form who I am.

Reaching back can mean resurfacing many painful memories, but it can also bring a sense of closure to many lingering feelings. Among some of my earliest and most profound experiences I can recall with any detail are few, but also very vivid. This still provides me a good rewind of what has helped me understand how and why I respond the way I do in various interactions. It helps me re-examine who I am and to rediscover the beauty and truth being withheld for so long.

Growing up, I can't say that I was very happy... nor if I knew exactly who I was and where I belonged. From early on, I was always thinking of pleasing others—my coach, teacher, parents, friends, employers, customers, or society overall. I knew who I was, but questioned if I was sick or wrong, simply because everyone else telling me I was. I knew that my inner self was trying desperately trying to make public and visible... to stop hiding! In those early years, this was probably the main reason I didn't smile much. Experiences from school to athletics to relationships to parenting to social engagements... each has their own separate, but distinct form of conduct and behavioral requirements, often a complete 180 from the identity I knew was mine. But where do I go to for help? And what I do ask them? There were no names or 'labels' for what I knew was very real. I am sure I would have been put away and labeled a 'freak'. But where would I go for friendship or personal confidence in a world that was built in a post WWII 'Stepford' mode. This was the age of denial, that in so many ways, manifested itself in so much societal unrest.

For me, 2013 was a whole new beginning—having seen the brightest light in my life, to date. My rediscovery of self is one of the guiding principles that has brought me to this point. It serves as the basis for who I am and WHY I am experiencing this renewal and liberation—something once very foreign to me. Creating this journal has been an immensely meaningful way to reflect, self-assess, and to cleanse my inner baggage. It has held me captive for much too long. This is a FAR better way to live in one's truth! With each of these chapter, my character took a series of major tests that I am meeting head on. But I also never thought anything would surpass these constant feelings of aloneness.

To put into perspective, since medical transition, my support system has undergone some change, some adding, others withdrawing their support putting me in a position of more 'self-reliance'. I have resigned myself to the probable fact that my children likely will never see (in person) or know their parent as she really is, nor will my brother—unless they ask(!). Although their withdrawal can be predictable—they too have a journey and one that is far different than mine, it has come at an expense and offers me little other choice. 'Perpetual tears' is no longer an option. God has demonstrated His love and strength in my character and my resolve to stay true to my mission.

Now, the progression of the next chapter of life will use these learnings, exposing me to new opportunities and challenges that will take this to a completely different level—AND to recommit that support to the LGBTQ+ community contributing any way I can. With ample history of experiencing shunning and support withdrawal from half a dozen missions and agencies over the last ten years, I am no stranger to the tears and trauma common to all of us in this community.

My love for those who care to join me on this journey and the bond we share supporting each other is what gives me strength and gets me through many days. And I want to be here for you as one more beacon of hope.

NEVER GIVE UP!
NEVER STOP LOVING!

DEDICATION

In honor and dedication to my two children whom I love beyond all measure. They have yet to learn who their father really is and who she has become. This book will give you some insight on the role you play in my life and the legacy of which we have all been blessed. And my eternal love and commitment to the Trans Community across the miles from every walk of life—you are forever celebrated!

TABLE OF CONTENTS

AN INTRODUCTION

My early years I spent questioning who I was surrounded by a 'loveless' family unit. There has to be more out of life—isn't there? At least that how I saw it. Spending countless hours training [in the water and on the pavement] is only one example that gave me a means to an end—but it was NOT the end. There was still something buried deep within me to be discovered if/when I chose to wake up—to begin to see things from a completely different vantage point. I take full responsibility for my interpretations of life lessons—that rests with no one or nothing else. To that end, this story will demonstrate how that worked in my life, and how I was destined to live a bit more unabashed—to stop hiding —and to finally BE that person whom I have always been.

Seeing my sister taken well before her time and watching the hospice caregivers look after my dying mother, helped plant a seed—to put some things in a clearer perspective. But there was much more, and certainly deeper yet to come. Where this was probably the straw that finally broke that elusive camel's back, these pages following will give you a better understanding hopefully of things you can relate, where YOUR life's experiences certainly contribute to the climax of YOUR story. At least this one does to my story. Packed with more than six decades of trials, trauma, and celebrations, each event provides useful learnings or guideposts to redirect or amplify my path eventually leading to a pinnacle decision. Likely, yours will compare in many ways. My hope is that you'll find some meaningful messages to apply in your journey.

It was clearly time for me to do something worthwhile, that would make a critical difference to many lives that would continue for a long time. It's easy to feel insignificant in this massive overpopulated and disconnected world bordering on an over-the-top society in every sense of the phrase. For years I remember saying to myself and others that when I did [this], I would contribute more. When I reached [this], I would volunteer more. That time will never come if I don't reconcile today with yesterday and move on. Living in the present is a vital message and take away from this reading. Please internalize this guidance for your benefit and your family and friends perhaps struggling with a revelation dealing with the Trans community. Those reaching out take a valiant step forward in establishing mutual ownership of learning and understanding those challenges confronting their loved ones. It is everyone's responsibility, mine included, to stay alert and well-informed—to push ahead for a role of advocacy demonstrating that unconditional love. We all share a role and a duty to offer guidance and support when the situation calls for it. This as much about YOU as it is about me.

In my world, how I have grown, how I live, and how I think is not dependent on any 'religion' as defined by so many in equally different ways. That philosophy and personal conviction is a very personal choice—and has saved me more than once from death's doorstep, some even from my own hands. This is an important point to make clear to readers and to be certain you understand that mine is not to sell you on any deity or religion. But to let you know how He worked in my life. Whatever way you choose to worship (or not) or to whom or how you address your prayer is of no one's concern but yours.

THIS 'OLD' HOUSE

It was great to finally settle down in a house that we could aptly name 'home'. Seemed like we were nomads early in my childhood having moved to six different addresses in three states in the first eight years of my life. My father changed employers regularly—not certain why, although I had my theories. It would be years before I finally discovered why but it was kept from the children of the family for most of my childhood.

Mom and I sat on the front curb to see the July 4th fireworks at the park many summers—and we could even hear the 'ooh' and 'ah' from the watchful crown in neighboring yards and a collective chorus from that single block away. After the festivities concluded, I remember catching my share of lightning bugs. What a joy! We would catch garter snakes and feed them flies from the creek at the park down the street. Pretty gory, but darn fun! Not so sure I grew up with a love of snakes, though. Au contraire'!

Summer of 1971, I took a job at the local pool coaching the age group swim team. On one momentous occasion, I must have forgotten to set the alarm to wake me for the 5:00 AM swim practice. Ten team members decided to walk the one block to my place to wake me up. Believe me, this was the start to the curse of my body clock waking me at 4:00 AM every day, a rock-solid behavior from that day forward.

Tech savvy dial phones were common of this day, ours with a party line when my dad and other neighbors would listen in. Never a private moment nor any ability to confer outside unless in person. Pretty tough to get a support system in those conditions. There was always a feeling of being watched by my parents to be sure their children did not stray from the strict code of conduct they demanded. And much of that was unwritten—but to be clear from the temper my father exhibited on what seemed like a daily routine against one or more members of the household—even my mother. Though I never witnessed his violence as such, I was a party to his 'spankings' that came most pronounced one day when I was found 'playing with matches' near the grade school I attended. A friend and I were attempting to light a punk to use a sparkler we had purchased for the pending July 4th celebration and parade in the area. A sixth grader discovered us and turned us over to our parents telling them "They were trying to burn down the school!" Without any desire to know the truth, my paddling proceeded with a typical parental remark *"This will hurt me more than it does you."* [Not so sure about that!]

In a massive six-bedroom split level house, eventually I slept in all five of them, but not my parents room—actually, my father didn't allow me in there ever and he made certain of that by locking the master bathroom just off their room entrance. Always wondered why, but not so sure I really wanted to know anyway. My dad ended up trashing the house before his death in 1995 after power and utilities were shut off 18 months earlier. My brother found his emaciated body sunken into his chair accessible only by a small path through the trash. I remember my sister taking a video of the house condition before being overhauled. I never saw it in person—and very thankful for that!

I remember moving into this house when it was first built in 1964, three months after JFK was shot, priced at $35,000. It was sold in 1997 after being rebuilt, for $150,000. Seems like a crime selling for so little—especially after the investments my parents had made hoping for retirement in Florida. My dad had a lifelong quest to expand his career path into real estate sales. Part of that extended into [now] country club lots he had purchased during WWII that was under development in the late 60's by a company that was later indicted for fraud, bilking many property owners of their lifelong savings and investments—my dad included. We discovered this when we arrived one Christmas break hoping to spend a relaxing week on the beach—something not done these days since all the property has now been bought privately or commercially. After a 1200-mile trip to southern FL, we drove into the drive of our villa that had not even broken ground yet—the contractor and developer had fled with our money and that of many others in the same boat. Another arrow in my growing 'distrust' quiver!

One of my fonder memories was Halloween—always a fun time! Popcorn balls and taffy apples were my favor-ites—before razor blades became a risk. How sick!? One year I got particularly inventive and went as Paul Revere (of the Raiders) by making my own costume. We were not allowed to buy costumes at the store and were forced to get imaginative. Actually, worked out pretty cool. Some friends and I assembled a makeshift rock band to resemble the group. Four of us fabricated a drum set and guitars out of cardboard and tape with magic markers. Pretty nice—at the time. My first real testament to 'trying on' a different look, albeit kind of lame too. I was a kid exploring youth. It was fun! But it also came with some substantial bullying from neighbor and school kids—seemed like this was just the beginning.

Growing up in a very white neighborhood in college town suburbia led to a lot of mis-truths in my childhood. Where I could easily have translated these as a misguided and indulgent member of society, I chose to question things from the start. I became a person of questioning, even in situations where some took major exception. In high school advanced algebra, I became confused with imaginary numbers. I had hoped to be a math major in college, but this was a pinnacle turning point in that decision. When asked of the instructor why $i2=-1$, he responded in anger with "That's just the way it is!" He later apologized for his abrupt remark but went on to explain that math is not something you can negotiate. That was a hard but very appropriate lesson to learn. It meant that I still tend to question everything—not just me.

I was very aware of my parent's bigotry, especially that of my father. His dislike for anything or anyone that was not a carbon copy of himself would not be tolerated. Clearly, that left me out of the picture. I learned early on that my father was an inspiration of what not to be in life. I am firmly convinced that if he were alive today, he would make certain that I was not. That innate feeling in me of his disinterest that became something near 'hate' in my later years was actually very well founded. This was my initial challenge of a trusting network that has been consistently absent. And those walls have become very real and very thick as time goes on demanding some persistent self-coaching and professional therapy—each has helped but is a constant internal struggle. However, it was clear to me even then that I am NOT my father's son!

Many memories (some good and more not so good) were pent up in this house most of which were trashed with the reconstruction. Not much more I care to remember or make you read here. But it is important to know that this was the source of much learning over the years that helped to form the character of who I have become.

GRADE SCHOOL

My earliest formative years in elementary school were relatively uneventful although enough memories too help put some things in perspective. From 1964 through a bachelor's degree was spent in this small Midwestern town, living in five different communities in three states between birth and third grade. There were difficulties for my father holding a job in those days, so we moved a lot.

This particular school was a central part of my youth 'education' from third to sixth grade. As marginal as many of those memories are, this will give you small window of highlights into a typical 'day in the life'-

- Each 4th grade pupil had a requirement to memorize 'Winken, Blinkin, and Nod' from start to finish as an assignment from my teacher, then we would be asked to recite a specific piece... but I was never called on. Equally as useless, was a year's assignment given the first day of class in late August to write out in numerical sequence 1—1,000,000 due the final school day. Seriously? For what objective did this serve? What a complete waste of time! And coming from the same teacher that gave everyone in the class an 'A' without any legitimate grading system or criteria. Is this how one gets on 'tenure'?

- My first crush! And in a pretty serious way, on my 5th grade teacher. Just not something I could shake, and to this day, she still has a place in my heart for her kindness, gentle demeanor, and presence. And just the beautiful scent of her perfume sent me into a spin. Definitely an impact!

- My parents reluctantly allowed me to play on 6th grade 'B' team in basketball and flag football. I was open to playing team sports but had no real allegiance or intent to pursue either beyond this introductory experience. Clearly, my talent was not here, evident in the selection to the 'B' teams—what was felt by my team mates as universal message of 'second class'. My only claim to fame was when I pulled the flag (football) on the opposing team's potential game-tying kickoff runback stopped him short at the five-yard line as time ran out. Phew! Other than relays in later years, this was the extent of my 'team' sports involvement. And I was quite okay with that.

- This experience rapidly confirmed my preference to individual sports, much more my thing when I experienced my first running event having lapped everyone else in the mile run. Probably the reason that became one of my favorite events in HS and college track. I recall in the late 70's having run an indoor half mile event against [then] the USA national record holder, and feeling a wonderful accomplishment simply staying on the same lap. What an experience! What a rush!

- Academically, I was no slouch, but also no brainiac or genius—hardly! I scored a 95 on the Stanford Achievement Tests (now more commonly referred to as the SAT-10). Not sure that did much more than provide an entry on the fictitious 'permanent record' that every teacher warned their students about. But it did help put me in some more advanced classes in my junior high school placements. What high marks I got, I worked hard for each. Nothing came particularly easy.

This was the age when it was acceptable for children to be taught half-truths or many 'facts' of history left untold or only partially telling of stories that drove some healthy misunderstanding to their pupils—a very incomplete viewpoint of American society's evolution—a curriculum in all school ages ripe with a curbed focus predominately on the white European perspective. The bulk of Black history, native American tribal nations, Hispanic, or any other culture or viewpoint seemed conveniently left out of their instruction leaving their pupils lives in a growing state of denial wrought with misinformation. Academic administration in my elementary and HS experience never seemed to focus their curriculum more current than the civil war—which conveniently left our critical

African American reality of slavery and bondage—that began at our 'colonization' of what we now call the USA. This type of subject has lost me my share of friends in the past, but I'm not ashamed and will not apologize. When asked if I would support 'rewriting history', my response follows—*"No, but I would support telling the truth. All of it!"* The schools I attended seemed to conveniently omit any mention of how some of our founding 'forefathers' owned slaves and supported the proliferation of the practice in colony development. And the outright theft of many territories and land then occupied by tribal nations was overlooked entirely. And although I support no specific political agenda, Al Gore had it right with his book titled *"An Inconvenient Truth"* about the denial of global warming and climate change developments. With age, hopefully comes wisdom...

Before HS, my only exposure to a non-white culture came when my father would host some of his students at the house for a final class together. I remember meeting several ethnic diverse members however without much significant interaction. Where I know my father made a point of inviting all participants to avoid indiscretion (or it may have been something the university administration required of him), I was never allowed much more than a brief greeting. But I did experience the physical differences and felt immense gratification knowing that there was something more to explore and to know much deeper.

The entire concept of LGBTQ+'s was never openly discussed or acknowledged as a real thing. I don't believe it even had a name except for those who chose to call it a sickness and "sexual diversion". There were no outlets for questions or counsel, no acknowledgement that there was a need for conversation, understanding and education. All those early feelings that I had and knew were very real had no means of exploring or understanding how they played into the bigger picture. My faith became a strong part of my early years only by virtue of listening to my heart. There were no opportunities to explore my knowledge base through a Google search or Facebook or any of the means we have today. No support groups, nothing. If one dared to bring it up even at this age, some would be marked for life. I knew no other road to take but inward. Again, another critical clue that I had to process carefully in my youth and well into adulthood to be certain I devoted the rest of my days seeking every truth I could find, not just my own. That is a common theme that resonates to me in my everyday life today.

MY HOME AWAY FROM HOME

The local city park was a familiar place in my childhood that was for all practical purposes, my home away from home where I spent the majority of my growing up experiences. I really had no parental coaching in much of anything, certainly not directed at my talents or interests, nor my thoughts and dreams or aspirations. None of that ever came up. In many ways, direct and indirect, I raised myself.

Certainly, my parents fed, clothed, and sheltered their children, but the majority of their person-to-person counsel was provided to my siblings. By the time I arrived on the scene, any actual direction short of barking orders at me to do chores or 'think of others, not yourself' was short in supply. My father was a renowned college professor and co-founder of the open classroom in teacher education. He had no interest in me as a person or certainly not as one of his offspring. By the time, the last child (me) was born, he had run dry on attention or love spent on the previous three. That became abundantly clear to me beginning with my first conscious understanding near my preschool years. I recall comments by each sibling in my adult years that our parents should be glad we turned out as well as we did given the complete lack of direction from either.

The park was a beginning to so many of my childhood memories, most of which I spent alone or in an individual activity—but as it turned out, was okay for most of the time. It was extremely easy to compare the park with my pastime representing a form of supervision or 'babysitting' by my parents. We took part in very few activities together and shared no interest in doing so.

I did have one 'best friend' who was with me in some ways through around 2009 until I came out to him—then the ties were broken never to hear from him again. I was devastated by his complete reversal of friendship—likely we both operated under completely different definitions of that term. But his influence on any part of my character or growth in my early years was negligible. It was the park and my desire to explore it that was a pivotal part of my memory. The impact on my adult life and that evolving in my adolescence and college life, this park played a critical role in many ways. Among my most enlightening moments are best described seasonally.

Summers—Days were consumed with swimming—learning, teaching, relaxing, and conditioning. And considering the park was only a block away, the convenience meant those summer days were 5AM to 9PM virtually every day. I learned to swim when I was seven years old, but not competitively until age nine. After taking swimming lessons to learn basic floating and freestyle, the rest was essentially up to me. I learned to favor my left side for breathing, including a technique used in fly. Eventually, I became well-versed in both sides, but my ambidextrous tendencies were just starting. My comfort level in the water, even at this age, was very apparent—I felt almost out sorts when I could not spend a few hours each day in the water.

To get some more advanced skills, there was marginal instruction available. Reading Doc Councilman's 'The Science of Swimming', I took copious notes and taught myself breast-stroke, backstroke, and fly, turns and starts, and learned some conditioning strategies and coaching skills by the age of 14. Our team won the local city championships twice in three years when I was their coach. I was also hired as a private instructor and condition coach for a preteen who later qualified for the Summer Olympic Games. In 1972, I followed my mentor to his home team to train for those Munich games, qualifying for a pretrial event in the 200 mt free en-route to a personal best. Training that summer with college men & women cov-ering 12—15K meters/day was a true test in a totally different way—provided a pinnacle change in my youth, setting me up for a major source of strengthening my resolve and character. The drive to get through that summer helped me mature in ways that has served me well into adulthood. The water had become my great equalizer.

In a world void of sound and noise, it was easy to get wrapped up in the serenity and peace that became a part of my daily routine from the moment I was introduced. When I was three years old, my mother allowed me to test the waters in a practice most would think bordered on cruelty. She would carry me in her arms to the middle of the pool in an area well over my head and let me go. Most might view this as a sink or swim moment, I suppose that would be a logical conclusion. But she knew me well enough that I was able to bob up and down enough to discover the air I needed to breathe was on top and lying on my back [then] was the easiest solution. After a few moments, that probably felt like hours to my mother, I stopped floundering and came to rest on my back. Odd as that was, in my adult life I am unable to float on my back at all without cheating (I recall passing my Red Cross Lifesaving & WSI exam by resting my right big toe on the bottom of the pool for the ten-minute back float test portion). My BMI only allows vertical floatation so that when my lungs exhale, I sink like a rock. This was my first open demonstration of comfort in this surrounding medium that gave me immense solace allowing a perfect environment for reflection and centering. Even offering a sense of flying where weight no longer is a concern, and balance and breathing becomes everything—all critical elements to my internal sense of peace. Almost a kind of rhythmic dance using the water and its physics to push and move me—that surrounds me with a cocoon of security. But I still had to learn how to tame it and use the power and forces where and how I could. This 'security' became my form of peace, when my persona was being questioned or threatened by other's reactions or behaviors, this was my perfect place to 'immerse' myself and become one with the water. It worked marvelously well!

But how does one choose and excel in something from which they are 'allergic'… at 10 years old, my body took exception to the unusually high concentrations of chlorine during an indoor 'backwashing' incident maintaining the pool system, and sent me into a fever of 104_0 F tailspin? After a 90-minute ice bath to recover and my first suppository (yay!), all is well. But very weird. My body's attempt at acclimating to the water of indoor pools. But I survived!

Summers were not just reserved for swimming, although with my sensitivity to excess heat and humidity typical of midwestern summers, running was a close 'second love' in my world. Preparing for the fall cross country season was always on my mind, especially as my tenure increased, so did the mileage—to a fault. After my freshman year, I was challenged with a new goal of being the #1 runner on the team that upcoming fall. And I had just learned about a special program where runners log their milage over the summer attempting a goal of 360 or 1000. In two of the three summers between HS years, I did one of each level, the 1000 completed just before my senior year—but got 'shin splints' as a result. Instead of entering the season in peak condition, I was injured nearly all of September. But I still managed a rewarding season with course record times. The park had become a multifunctional place of activity and solace.

<u>Spring and Fall</u>—When I was ten years old, I got super excited about entering a local kite flying contest. Using the open fields at the park where we ran our cross-country course around was a great site to host this first-time event. I had made my own delta shaped version of a kite with a bedsheet tail for balance. I was infatuated at the time with Wonder Woman and Captain America, so it seemed appropriate to fashion the kite with the look and color scheme of Captain America's shield.

Pretty impressive if I do say so myself! It was accompanied by a self-made wooden hand-crank reel that held one mile of heavy-duty kite string. My brother made a box kite from pre-cut sticks, wood glue, and grocery bags for paper. On the morning of March 15th (contest day), we tested our works and skills before the scheduled 2:00 PM official start. During our warmups, the breeze was simply perfect—just enough to get mine aloft in seconds and before we knew it, all we could see was a faint bow upward in the sky from which the entire reel was spent. Never having this kind of success before, I misjudged the time needed to bring it back in time for the 2:00PM start. I had no idea how much work it took to bring it in against the updraft—it really took a physical toll on me, but I was able to regain full control and got ready for the start. BUT... with less than 10 minutes remaining to get things airborne, I couldn't duplicate my earlier feat in warmups and had to forfeit. ARGH! Major disappointment! On a good note, at least my brother won best box kite! That was very cool!!

Many of my fall memories consumed with running cross country. Although this annual exercise started my freshman year, it became an annual ritual. Taking a jaunt through the countryside, wherever that may be, with the changing foliage and smell of the fall always took me back to this time. In as much as this has some odd sense of power over me, even that fall after my high school graduation when I took a job with a painting crew, I really missed what had become an annual event. So much that I left my would-be career and re-entered school in January that winter for college. At the time, that is where I knew I had to be.

My freshman year of HS, the course we ran at this park was 2.75 miles but was eventually changed to 3.15 the next year—more than I had ever run in a race in my life and was not entirely sure I could. But that changed. Quickly! I had shown the rest of the team that I meant business and I was out to take on even the finest runners and upperclassman. But I also discovered how those tables turned during my junior and senior years. There will always be someone ready to take my place. My resolve proved a valuable asset becoming varsity and a letter winner all four years. This park was home to some of the greatest races and most personally challenging moments. It's funny what you discover deep down when you are put in a position to reflect on your limits and capabilities.

My running coach was not a particularly good coach. In his day, he was once a gifted sprinter on the track but failed miserably at coaching and at working with young prodigies. And because of his tenure and experience at both running and teaching, he was well respected. Few questioned his methods or his character—a clear indication to those on the team that his command of respect had little basis besides his 'type A' personality and his age and experience. These days, it's highly unlikely his methods would have been tolerated by any parent or assistant coach witnessing his practices and how he belittled and openly humiliated his subjects. His style was one of 'reverse psychology' as he referred it. He purposely would verbally abuse and tear down various members of the team. And I seemed to be the target of his greatest attacks—according to another assistant coach because he thought that I had the most promise that justified his attacks. His logic was intended to make teammates angry and want to prove him wrong, and his failure to see the detrimental impact that stayed with me all four years of high school. And that was also multiplied by four additional seasons each spring on the track. He was even known to have used the loudspeaker in the press box during practice on our track to publicly call out his remarks. And because the sound carried, one could hear his open disgust for blocks away. That would follow me into my class schedule the next day serving more public embarrassment. I guess what doesn't kill you only makes you stronger!?

Even after all these past years, I still remember the names and schools of my arch-rivals in all three sports I practiced in high school. I was good friends with all of them and shared deep respect with their ability and character. That was important. Arch—rivals are not intended to detest rather we shared a common bond, for the sport and for each other. It also made for a sense of purpose at each race knowing they were there and providing a huge incentive to perform. For each encounter, most races concluded with a personal best time for me—a tribute to the respect I had for each of them. I soon discovered that my satisfaction of self-performance was best when I was competing in these rivalries. In virtually every city we traveled for swimming or running events, I knew of someone I shared a common bond and admiration but also wanted desperately to beat. With most of them, we traded victories back and forth over our careers.

Winter—In the middle of the upper Midwest, it is hard to consider any outdoor winter sports that had a special attraction in my youth. I probably would have taken on cross country skiing had I known it existed. But all we had available was ice skating to which I took a direct liking. Each winter the park administration would flood the basketball court right outside the fenced in pool area and wait for Mother Nature to do her thing. Thanks to the massive curbing the park administration installed around the courts, they were able to seal the rain drains and flood the area creating a 30-inch-thick sheet of ice welcomed patrons of all ages. This is where I learned to speed skate in a very confined area not known for extensive sprinting capabilities. So, I was challenged with learning how to pick-up speed and brake very quickly because the ice was about to end.

Two weeks in a row, I learned the hard way. I had some difficulty learning the long blades of a speed skate making it easy to trip over myself. The first time, I took a dive landing chin first resulting in eight stitches. Where this would not have been more than a flesh wound, I learned a valuable lesson how to be a patient with patience. One week later, I was released by the doctor too resume skating, with the understanding I would be extremely careful and avoid re injuring myself. Famous last words! This time double the stitch amount and one month off the ice. Oh well, this just added to my resolve—I eventually moved my enjoyment of speed skating into an indoor hockey rink.

The park was my respite and became a place where even today when I return to the area, it calls me back. A time when it was something expected to do—to dream and to challenge one's character. As I did. There were many moments where I applied these learnings from this park and the source of growth and peace it gave me... use this life to reach out to others especially those sharing your interests. Finding a common bond is often the start of a lasting friendship. But don't be resistant to sharing of yourself. That's a lesson I learned probably too late although better late than never. There is a strong balance between calculated risk and reward. No one ever grew without taking risk.

Coming to terms with my own shortcomings and character flaws has been a lifelong challenge, especially those with both inherent and learned tendencies. My OCD has often taken over in the absence of a trustworthy network of support, but also tends to keep me from 'stepping back' and allowing those deserving of that trust to have mine. Everyone deserves that chance.

Take a look deep within to confront your innermost values. Always try to seek to understand FIRST. Ask yourself some critical questions, to make a commitment to never give up, no matter what the task or who is asking. Stay true in your central values—never allow anyone to keep you from pursuing a dream. And NEVER allow someone to steal your drive to serve their own agenda.

THE QUAD

Came to be known simply from the four major streets that define central campus, I recall after riding to college campus where my mom worked, then hoofed it across the famed quad to my high school about a mile total. As historic memories dictate, I remember the world's tallest dorm being built and shortly after opening day for the ribbon cutting ceremony someone took a dive off the 18th floor, apparently testing gravity. And on one of these trips, I was offered some 'grass' as I unknowingly walked through on my way to high school amidst a rock festival called the 'Rites of Spring 1971'. Wow—quick flashback! The more things change, the more they stay the same. Seemed just like a mini-Woodstock; REO Speed wagon and Golden Earring were two of those bands that played till late hours most of one week in April that spring. And the pungent odor of pot smoking was very apparent as I made my way across campus. This was my first meet of what could be described as a midwestern gathering of concertgoers, potheads, and hippies, but also from a student population openly reminiscent of a Forest Gump rally. Fascinating! One example of keynote history I was witnessing, even amongst anti-Vietnam demonstrations too. Might have been fun to take part—but not something that had entered my mind, yet.

During my freshman year at college, one day en-route to a class on 'History of European Art', my brother and I rode our bikes to campus, normally each day at 8:00 o'clock for first hour classes. But on this particular day, I was confused and was heading to the opposite side of campus—I was supposed to be going to Tuesday classes on a Wednesday, the wrong side of campus. For some very odd reason, I quickly glanced back behind me to see if I could turn, to verify that no oncoming cars were encroaching. I saw a VW bug two blocks away and figured I had ample time. Pulling a U-turn just in time, I glanced behind and I could see that I was about to be hit. Next thing I know, I am on a gurney in the ER. My brother said my body flew about 20 feet and broke the VW windshield on impact—seriously?

After a brief verification of my vitals, I was released to return to classes. And just in time to ace the midterm! All good, but my bike was totaled. No legal charges either way! And although shock hit me later that afternoon and was out of commission for two days, this is one of at least six lives I have used so far.

KNOCKING ON DEATH'S DOOR? NOT YET!

Where this was the first time that I can recall with any significant detail, there certainly were several other situations, of which we have all probably experienced at one time or another. All I know is that with each incident, it was noticeably clear to me that a power far greater than me intervened—and thankfully so. Over the years, I can recall some key events where He lifted me from the grips of death.

My first year of high school track put me on the varsity squad. This required considerable mileage in most afternoon practice sessions. Before each session began, we were asked as a team to sit in the hallway right outside the locker room next to the outside door leading up to the track. That door offered a significant blind spot to the left side when exiting. Unknown to anyone on the track team, the baseball team had decided to place its automatic pitching machine directly in that blind spot aiming its pitches in front of the doorway. No signs, no instructions, and no catcher. Just high velocity automated throws against a blank wall. In my competitive nature, I burst out the door when someone yelled "Watch out!" I turned my head to the left as I ran past, seeing ball come directly at me with only enough time to turn my head, striking me just above my left ear and knocked me cold. After being rushed to the hospital, I came to with no major residual effects besides a concussion and facial bruising. Doctors said that, had the impact been .5" closer to the temple, I probably would not have lived. And I should expect continued migraines for several more years. Another close call!

After spending the majority of my growing years in the plain states, it was especially odd moving north when my love of the ocean, swimming and outdoor running transplanted me in a much colder climate. I also discovered kayaking on the nearby river, and downhill skiing… but not without some growing pains. The highest point in the area was also a state park and a ski hill recently under new management. Their quest for expansion was not bound by much more than those state park limitations and some local resident dissention. I now had a bona fide way to enjoy winter months in a downhill play area within a day's drive. Wonderful! Another way to recapture my solace in a winter setting—actually had a very tranquil touch of its own very similar to the water in the pool. When atop the highest peak, one could see for miles and take in the grandeur of how vast the world really is. Really fit well in fulfilling my place for peace and centering.

Much of that peace was shattered one fateful evening under the lights on one of their new expansion runs groomed with 'man made' snow, ironically named 'Superstition'. And with January temperatures often exceeding 0ºF, the ice crystals from their snow machines made some of the runs almost bald from the lack of natural powder to carve and slalom. As I hit one of those famed ice spots on a near 45-degree slope, I could not recover and took off into the trees on the western boundary. That was one of the compromises the state had made with the expansion to avoid trimming or removing too many trees. That meant there was no alternative but to collide with one, head-first. As a result, I broke two facet joints in three separate vertebrae, two of which were in the cervical area, and a rib came dangerously close to rupturing my spleen.

When I recovered consciousness, I went through the normal bodychecks one would attempt after blacking out—looking up at the night sky, it sure looked like heaven, but I knew better... it was <u>way</u> too cold. Then I wiggled my toes to be sure I felt movement. But wow did my back hurt when I tried to sit up! My son was on his snow board at the time, and quickly came over to assess the situation. Yelling for the ski—patrol, a sled took me to the warming house. When I was able to move to the car, we proceeded to the hospital when the pain was bad enough to even remove my boots. I was admitted with an immediate MRI and a serious dose of morphine (Wow! Did that put me out for the evening!). All told, a compressive fracture did not require surgery, but still had to wear a corset for six weeks. Rating the pain would easily rank a 15 on a 1-10 scale, but nothing compared to childbirth—for that, I am sure. NOW I wear a helmet every time I ski!

The morning after my first night in the hospital, the morphine had definitely worn off and the reality of the pain was now abundantly clear. After the nurse came in to check on me, I asked when I could plan to be discharged, to which she replied, *"When you can walk!"* That's all I needed to hear to get motivated. Although the pain was far too much to endure to even move to the edge of the bed, I was apparently provided with an adjustable bed giving me an elevated capability I could not do on my own. By early evening that day I was able to walk with the help of the adjustable bed getting me to a position where I could grab on to a railing and stand erect. As painful as that was, I preceded to shuffle about the room as awkward as I could.

The second morning, I was able to replicate this process enough to walk to the nurse station but with the pain ranking somewhere around 8. Not a lot better, but enough to allow a full discharge by 3:00 PM that Sunday. They prescribed a corset that I had to be wear 24 x 7 for six weeks (or until the doctor said otherwise). And because that made business travel almost impossible, I was destined to spend the next few months at home. The downside from all of this was a constant need to keep myself physically fit even with age. It also helped my back alignment and residual pain wearing heels, but mostly done so at church and formal occasions. But this began a church stigma of wearing heels-something I will unlikely ever live down.

Then in the late summer of 2011, I was faced with one of the most humbling experiences that tested both my character and my resolve. I was outed by my ex, forced to confront my truth in front of our attorneys during my divorce deposition proceeding. I had been unaware that photos on my computer were being breached, as much as my trust. There's no one to blame but myself. When I saw the photos, I was quite relieved, smiled welcoming [her] completely. She was no longer buried, and she yearned for exposure. I am sure my children did not know where to turn or what questions to ask, but I still felt complcte betrayal by both, neither having spoken with me about anything. Despair and withdrawal consumed me like a blanket of darkness—something only those of similar situations can fully grasp. But I had no one to talk with or trust… more of my testaments to abandonment and confusion that added to this growing wall of isolation. Where was that love that I was told I had? This is when I needed it so desperately. SO MUCH and RIGHT NOW! I began contemplating ending this seemingly endless circle of despair and searched online for a solution to make this nightmare stop once and for all. To support my decision, it seemed best to look for a high point north of my place where the terrain was hillier and rockier, where I could speed over the edge without a guardrail and avoid hurting anyone or anything in my path to the end. That would be it! Done! No more pain, no more loneliness.

No sooner had I made that decision and preparing a means to follow through leaving parting gifts as best I could, my phone text alerted me—just as my pen was hitting the paper. It was my son. He asked if there was an opportunity to meet sometime before he left for fall semester to "get something off my chest". It was at that meeting he confessed he was the one who discovered the photos and failed to confront me about them first. *"Will you find a way to forgive me, Dad?"* To which I quickly shot back, *"OMG, absolutely and always! Never doubt that for a moment!"* Assuring him of my unconditional love, I threw my arms around him and hugged him with all my might, tears flowing from both of us. Just then, my daughter arrived home. I launched from my seat, running down the stairs to greet her, more tears followed asking for her forgiveness. This pulled me back from the depths of sorrow and a place of darkness I never want to experience again…And a better perspective of the questions I know they still have never asked me.

After moving to my current home in 2013, fate would have it that I met another special friend who I can truthfully say saved my life one fateful evening. I was invited to a weeknight dinner celebrating friends. And the hostess was serving a beautiful top sirloin that continues to challenge my commitment only to fish and chicken. Having given up beef from my diet several years ago, I was not very fluent in gaging the size of my bites. And mis-judging the density of one particular bite demanded far more chewing to change that 'glob' into something capable of being swallowed. After several unsuccessful attempts to dislodge the bite, my new 'friend for life' looked over at me when I gave him the sign 'cutting my throat'. His quick action hoisted me out of my chair, moved me into the bathroom close by, and began to perform the Heimlich maneuver. All this time, I tried profusely to get any semblance of breath, but none was to be had. Seven massive chest pulls, one after the other, proved unsuccessful. This went on for 90 seconds until #8, up and out the chunk of beef flew into the bathroom sink. Nothing compares with the fear when trying desperately to get a breath—but nothing at all, not even a gasp for each attempt and I was growing blue-faced quickly. Although I remained relatively calm through all this, I could only think during that 90 second nightmare was *"Really? Is this how I'm going to die? I can see the headlines now." Where's the Beef!"*. Although I still am drawn to the delightful aroma of a juicy Porterhouse on an outdoor grill, this incident has led to a re-removal of beef from my daily diet—and a suitably bruised rib—I quickly welcomed as a cost I was very willing to pay.

Valentine's Day 2014; While driving a friend's [suspect] van in a major snowstorm, I spun a 720 in the median at 1:00 AM landing softly in a cushion of snow without colliding with anything or anyone. I had religiously checked the forecast for a storm that was expected to travel squarely in the middle of my trek back. I was hoping to outrun the storm track after leaving my Mother's duplex. My brother, sister and I were trying desperately to vacate our Mother's home who had died two months earlier, by the end of February to avoid an unoccupied rental. Filling the van with a sleeper sofa and bookcase made the vehicle quite heavy and especially difficult to handle in treacherous conditions.

I was watching the storm progress across the central plains and knew the window of opportunity was closing quickly… and that if I chose to wait it out, I risked having to stay the next week or two when the forecast was warmer, and snow accumulations would start to thaw. But the storm also gave my drive a very short window of time in which roads could be clear and reliable. Ultimately, the National Weather Service was predicting 18" by late the next morning. With clear roads starting out, I traveled quickly up to 45 miles west of my destination before conditions were steadily getting way beyond control. Like many have come to experience, this is what I affectionately refer to as 'white knuckle driving'. At 10 minutes into the new day, I was deep in ice-covered pavement with snow-pack on top, making sudden maneuvering something very likely would send me into a spin. Just then, a passing motorist misjudged the ice and spun out in front of me creating my need to turn slightly to avoid hitting them— BUT that was enough to send me into a two complete turns and landing precariously in the center of the median—in a pillow of fluffy white stuff amazingly untouched and unharmed. Less than five minutes passed when a policeman stopped to ask me if I was hurt. I was so relieved and rolled down the window to speak with the patrolman, explaining *"Yes, but I think I may have wet myself!"* He kindly summoned a wrecker who was in the area pulling out countless others with much the same situation.

The rest of the trip took me 3 1/2 hours to cover the remaining 45 miles arriving at home by 4AM with semis zipping by me with little regard for the conditions and some shoulder drop offs that would be something no one would recover if they went over the edge. When I arrived, I was greeted with 18" of fresh snow in my serpentine driveway demanding another hour of manual shoveling to get into my garage. THIS was a night to forget, but also to be thankful I was alive.

Where my life has been spent largely alone, some by choice but most as a survival instinct, I've grown used to the concept of self-coaching. I still have much to learn—my tendency still to withdraw and seek that inward counsel tends to shut others out. A major discovery is the value of outreach and a sense of community that cannot be overstated. There are so many who genuinely want to help and to love—just as I want to receive that love, and I have to be willing to be vulnerable and share mine—always!

Everyone goes through various forms of trauma in their lives, most far worse than any I could imagine. I don't believe that I will ever go through anything I can't handle even at the depth of question, reason, or logic. But even these have only been a fraction of the trauma and liberation of my transition I have experienced. Finally, some critical things were becoming clearer. Each brush with death had given me a renewed perspective with greater vision of my purpose. I was not nearly done yet, and there was still substantial work to be done.

SURF AND TURF
(THE POOL AND THE TRACK)

At the age of 9, I fell in love with water and anything aquatic. As I gravitated to individual sports and the technical side of art (drafting), neither particularly interested either parent. My hope was to be worthy of their love, respect, and attention—somehow. In those years before I graduated from college, my quest was successfully complete but only in my own world. I recall only one cross-country race my father attended, my mom never. Neither attended track or swimming events unless my brother was also competing. And neither parent nor anyone in the family knew or acknowledged my 1972 landmark time trial for Munich. I quit caring or trying anymore to get their attention, but now it became a huge burden on myself from myself. This was among the most profound revelations that living up to everyone else's expectations was not something worth constant pursuit, that would be my demise if I let it. My immersion into swimming and running was my solution for therapy, for discernment just to sort out who I really was and what I had to do to survive. Feeling like an outsider in my own family and at school put me at odds with many relationships—always distrusting at the start and constantly questioning my self-worth. Both sources of the track and the pool offered solace in a contemplative space that no one could assault or intrude.

Growing up being largely invisible to my family was probably THE one challenge I could never overcome. My biggest aspiration at the age of 14 was to be noticed by my parents, acknowledged for some element of love expressed in words or of some actual demonstrated interest. My brother was an obvious example of what they emulated in him. He was everything to them that I was not; and because I knew even then of my tendencies (I prefer to think of them as early markers of my true gender), clearly, I was the black sheep of the three previous perfect siblings. I had all the earmarks of an outcast, later confirmed in writing when my father sent me a letter on May 24th, 1988 informing me how he had "… never wanted your birth…" and "… you were a mistake to be born at all" and "you would never earn [his] love!" Pretty direct and harsh, but one of many pieces of the puzzle that all came together…eventually.

My two older sisters were musicians and artists, both prodigies of liberal arts -primary reasons that each would be attending a prep school designed for such budding talent. Since my father was a professor of music, this fit right in with his perfect offspring as legacies he valued above most anything or anyone else. My brother drew a slightly shorter straw and the two of us were destined for a cross town school that we both preferred, but the parental move was very evident and strategic. My brother excelled in woodworking and building trades for which my father also demonstrated some talent. So, the mold was cast; and so were the expectations!

My father regularly reminded me of my illness and any tendency or misbehavior was openly shared with the family intended to publicly ridicule and humiliate me. Trying to negotiate the purpose of a jockstrap in my pre-teen years was one trauma I try to forget. Asking the question of my father what it was for and the purpose of the 'cup' that came with it drew his laughter first, then his ire and disgust—again, another reason to avoid coming to him for any question or issue, certainly reason to withhold my growing distaste for anything male. This was not the era where one could 'Google' and find answers at lightning speed. [Guess the cup wasn't supposed to be a respirator after all!] I grew more and more introverted with more anger directed at my parents vented on my opponents in the water and on the track. My critique of my own performance became an active part of me to this day. The upside? Whatever talent I had proved to be a relentless attribute. In the water, I became a machine piling up wins like wrestlers measure their wins & losses. Each time upon my return home from an event, my parents would ask how I did? When I informed them of my places and times I achieved, my father's response was *"It figures"*, not even looking up from the book being read. Clearly, my journey was of no interest to anyone but me.

High school track and cross country were much the same with my two early years shared with my brother's later years. High on my list of priorities then was to beat him on both venues, one of which was achieved in a home track meet in my freshman year. We both traded positions every lap of the two-mile race, until a quick burst sent me past his shoulder on the final curve. On the way by he uttered the words *"Oh, nice move!"* It was only the assistant coach who then said to me *"Now that you've beaten your brother, what's next"?* This pivotal achievement was my challenge to look way beyond this present world to recognize and live my truth everyday stronger and more profound.

'Next' by my definition was still 13 months away when I spent the summer of '72 training for the Olympiad. But before '72 preparations, I still had some major work to do. During the summer of '71, I discovered a blend of swimming and running conditioning that proved to be a good compliment to each other and allowed an equally good opportunity to enjoy some variety. The downside? My feet took quite the beating from staying soft in the water and the trauma from road mileage created frequent blood blisters—painful and time-consuming to heal, especially trying to harden the skin when the water did just the opposite.

During the summer before my senior cross-country season, I spent training for what I had hoped would be a landmark performance by logging 1000 miles of roadwork—a feat that would prove not such a wise move from seriously painful shin splints. The only way to repair this condition is to not run. A recent study in the Journal of Sports Medicine and Physical Fitness indicates that this condition affects about 13% of all running injuries. But this would also be my first exposure, after swimming, to shaving my legs, in preparation for a special way to tape the shins. Learning from the team trainer, I used a weave method to support the calf muscle from the repeated pounding on hard surfaces that caused this inflammation. I was able to recover enough to perform a personal best and having gained the number one varsity position, captain, and MVP. Beating the seniors was everything, especially two years later when the new Frosh began beating me! VERY humbling, indeed!

In swimming, during those years, it was customary to shave all of the body that had exposed hair short of the scalp itself. But there were some who even shaved their head mostly to gain a psychological advantage, or so they thought. There would also be some swimmers who decided to add a layer of oil or Vaseline to their skin reducing the coefficient of friction in the water. Research showed that had no effect and was actually prohibited in sanctioned events. [A point worth noting as learned from shaving experience, there is no significant pressure needed on a fresh blade. As obvious as that may sound today, it wasn't so back then. My first experience on my shins drew some serious blood. OMG did that hurt!]

When June of '72 arrived, so had my dreams—at least with the hopes to progress from a 'nobody' to a real contender and in some races, maybe even a favorite. Working out in a practice circle with college swimmers demanded a special degree of tenaciousness and drive—they were 21 and 22, and I had just turned 16. And with six to seven hours of water time per day and teaching swim lessons for four, besides eating and sleeping and the occasional eight-mile bike ride back to the coach's place, there was little time for much else. I knew exactly why I was there, and I was determined to make the best of it. And if I could attract a positive response from my parents, all the better. But quite frankly, that was the farthest thing from my mind.

On the final week of the '72 summer season, before college classes resumed, two of my new elder circle mates decided to take me out to break my alcohol-virginity. Being the youngest of four and clearly the black sheep, I was quite socially naive. After draining an entire bottle of Strawberry Hill, we all decided to see a movie, but not before a visit to Mr. Quick. This is where I learned to avoid mixture of some food items with alcohol. As much as I like the idea of a strawberry milkshake, that was <u>not</u> a smart move. It did sound good at the time, but little did I realize the sweats I experienced in the theater was foretelling of my unloading all over my college teammates. Quite the gross sight and fragrant smell, no doubt, but well deserved for my escorts. They promptly dumped me in their car backseat and went on to finish their evening's entertainment—and probably to help clean up the mess I made. After sleeping it off that night, each participant in the evening's events suffered from an immense hangover—except me. That was the best workout I ever had—and with better than race times between intervals. I know that our coach was puzzled—but we each smiled and claimed ignorance. That was telling enough. I know he knew!

That summer's highlight was a personal best 1:51.10 for the 200-meter freestyle which became my favorite event, but not quite good enough for the Munich games. Again, my goals were still exceeded that summer and prepared me for a lot of future challenges, many of which are life lessons and demonstrated the value of living in the present. Most of my truth was still waiting for discovery. One day—among my greatest dreams—was to swim in my true self, feeling the caressing water around my 'transformed' body after GRS became a reality 44 years later.

The following winter swimming season in high school from that summer training for Munich, was particularly difficult. Our new coach had replaced one who had just left the teaching profession leaving this position vacant. The danger of canceling the season was very real without his intervention. However, everyone on the team quickly discovered that he had no experience and no background in competitive swimming. He later admitted he couldn't even swim. Once again, I was faced with the decision to self-coach or seek some other means of helping the team as best I could. No longer would it be enough just to compete, but now it seemed the right thing to do to give my novice coach the journal of workouts I had kept that summer. On the surface, that seemed like a fair trade. However, I was not thinking clearly that this may be something that was not welcome. My role quickly moved to that of consultant when asked and began swimming events that were not my favorite simply because we had a limited roster many of whom could not swim the longest or hardest events. Most athletes will agree that one usually chooses either short or longer distances with which to specialize. With my preferences as sprinting events, I was also entering the longer and multiple stroke events just to fill the quota and avoid forfeiting races. This continued for the next two seasons before graduation since I was only one of two in my class on the team.

Another critical lesson I learned through all of my swimming years took hold after the summer training. Now that I was at least in contention for every race I entered, my goal was not to beat the person next to me, or the fastest seed in the heat—that was the customary reason for stacking all the fastest in the last heat and in the center 2-3 lanes. As a general rule, the outside lanes made it virtually impossible to judge your speed by the fastest entry simply because you could not see them that far away. But if your focus is where it should be, you'll win no matter what. My attention was fixed on beating the clock. Nothing else mattered. In heats where I was seeded as a top entry, I often requested the side lane because I did not want people using me to judge their speed. I knew exactly what I was doing—and with very few exceptions, it worked!

My senior year was less focused on pinnacle achievements in the water or on the track. My consciousness was more directed at a growing female awareness and studying my own behavior, reactions and responses, interests, and interactions with others. Much maturity was gained here mostly from simple observations and trying to sort out why some of my mannerisms and preferences were the way they were. I recall entering the summer's 4H County Fair with my open recipe of fried chicken, the only thing that I really knew how to make very well. But I will say it rivaled local restaurants which at the time was quite good. And in customary fashion, I was becoming more frequently content at being totally alone in a crowd.

Every new year's growth was full of more instances of questioning feelings and confronting my own gender certainty. There were no names or categories I could put myself into, although countless times my father tried. I was routinely informed of my sickness and my perversion trying on my sister's clothes and underwear, as it had nothing to do with a sexual outlet. I needed to see in the mirror who I felt I really was. No excuses—simply fact. But not of something my parents were willing to change their mind. Facts were not important with them—that became another of my painfully obvious tenants within which I had to live.

Living up to anyone's expectations, even as difficult as it was with my parents and siblings, was a losing battle from start to finish. That took me nearly a lifetime to figure out. To this day, I still visit my parent's niche at the Memorial Gardens in my hometown during the Christmas season to pay my respects hoping for some closure. They never really knew me and never wanted to, least not in the truth I have always known. That became painfully obvious to me when I read my father's letter in 1988.

Individual teaching and coaching moments are many if we only take the time to see and listen. Offering our support through unconditional love should start at a young age to help build out our immense character through adult life. I hope that is one of my strongest legacies I leave. And choosing to live on my terms has taken me decades to learn, the liberation and complete peace it has given me has saved me more than once from the grips of death. My childhood quest for attention—simply just being noticed by my parents paid little dividends, however, it did a means to understand my character and to form the basis of who I've become. For that alone, I would trade none of it.

GETTING IN THE ZONE

Swimming and track, both being individual-based sports, allowed me a unique way to excel and center. Certainly not unique only to these sports, many athletes find themselves performing best in practice [and on race day] at a level a champion enjoys simply because they're ultra-focused. This is what many, me included, refer to being "in the zone". In my world, my psyche generally began an evening ritual well before race days to help get me ready for the 'zone'.

Depending upon the venue, I would often visit the pool site the evening before race day. I definitely favored long course versus short. This automatically meant fewer turns and more importance on alpha count and cadence. Alpha count referred to the number of cycles per stroke in a given lap (one length of the pool). For my count, a long course race (a 50-meter pool) in which a 1500 meters race meant a sustained cadence of 16 alpha cycles per lap. The more cycles, generally the more one fatigues and slower the pace. The longer the race, the more critical the sustained count. Cadence was slightly different, but still a critical measure of rhythm and balance in the water—one could even equate this as a 'dance' of sorts. How the stroke splits the water in a smooth entry, fully extends an efficient pull, and the body's roll side to side allowing full extension of the shoulders as far and deep as possible in every cycle. My coach taught me to visualize drawing a question mark with each hand beginning with the outstretched arm at the full body roll position, drawing a backwards mark with the left hand. This was mechanically the best way to assure the most efficient pull possible. Not sure that is still taught today, but it certainly worked for me!

In my freestyle, breathing became the single most important aspect—of which only rigorous conditioning would provide. As a rule, I breathed on both sides once every three pulls, but favored the left side. Just became more comfortable with a natural tendency of my body to pull slightly out of alignment when breathing on the right side—this would cause my torso to drop too much and increased drag, something critically important to avoid. No breath into the turns and none out until three alpha counts off the wall. That was my formula to resume the next lap with the 'wake' bouncing off the wall, carrying me with it as much as possible. Too slow a turn or a breath right out would miss that return wake and it would pass right by me. And a breath too early after the turn also meant the head tends to go up, the body down, requiring much more energy to get closer to the surface—drag! This became a crucial strategy in all events, not just the sprints. That approach, sustained throughout a longer race, might be just the ticket with a 'touch out' finish in micro-seconds. Conditioning meant up to 7-8000-meters per workout, sometimes twice a day totaling over 14,000 meters. Most of which were directed at peak season workouts deigned to 'tear down' each of us, working to a tapered format closer to key race dates. In short, putting each swimmer in the best possible condition at the best possible time to get the best possible results.

I would rehearse the race in full standing on the blocks for the race I was about to undergo and in the lane I would be assigned. Perhaps that metaphor (staying in your lane) rings true right about now.

[At what point would I get out of my comfort zone and explore the truth I knew was mine but still in an environment that demanded strict conformance to other's expectations? Quite the paradox! I would think through the entire race, simulating my anticipated experience hopefully, netting a win!]

On race-day, things generally went pretty much as planned—but not always. At home meets, most things were much more predictable because of familiarity of the water, the walls and marking of lane path and width, starting blocks, etc. As the captain of our HS team and age group coach, we dreamt up the idea of taking a container of our own pool water labeled "home team" and ceremoniously dropping it in our visiting team's pool giving us an equal home team advantage—or so we thought. If that seems like a weak message, the kids loved it. And that's all that counts! But getting used to those lane markings and sizes are supposed to be uniform dimensions and configurations, although not all pools and athletic directors practiced the same level of diligence, especially in high school meets. At least two of those on our schedule still used older pools (we would affectionately refer to as 'bathtubs') in which they measured 20 yards vs 25 yards (5 laps to a 100 vs 4 laps).

This meant that some races, especially those of greater distance were likely to produce faster times since more turns usually means greater advantage with more push-off opportunities to gain momentum—four turns vs. the typical three in a 100-yard sprint. In my freshman year, I swam the 400-yard free that was later changed to the 500. But that year, in a 20-yard pool, I was able to come within 14 seconds of the state record—a feat that became a school record never broken since the event was never performed in sanctioned meets after that.

When it actually came time for the race, nerves were at their highest. But a traditional pre-meet meal of bananas and peanut butter usually put me at ease. Sometimes even a hard-boiled egg or two would add to the stomach without being too much or loading me down. One learns over the years what works and what doesn't. As much as I like spicey foods, that can send an upset stomach into overdrive within the first 100 of a 1500 meter race. When the electronic start signals, we are off, and the fight begins. In the side lane, when I am blessed with that vantage point, my rhythmic pace begins in a ritual that mirrors most practice drills—but THIS time is for real. My first breath comes when I break the water after nearly 20 meters from the dive. The water is a comforting pillow around me, but not to take for granted... losing that cadence often means finding water to take in vs. air. And the pace of 33 second splits each lap is my goal that will assure me a personal best time-IF I can keep it up. But this is also my customary time to drift into a trance—a controlled mindset where my 'auto pilot' takes over from the conditioning of the past few months. My conscious thoughts begin a conversation with myself focusing on emptying my mind from the noise on the pool deck right now and the fervor of the race itself, feeling my breathing in a rhythmic cadence. It is my push that keeps me striving to stay within its power. Lap after lap, split after split, turn after turn, my alpha count increases slightly, but enough to bring me back to reality and realizing I am within a few meters of the gun lap, my hands fighting off the tingling sensation of oxygen debt—I am in the final stages of the race and my physical limits. I dig into my heart and my core, as deep as I know can. My pulls increase in power and exaggerate my body roll to stay in sync with my breathing sequence. As the end approaches off the final turn, my heart pounding, I search for the last ounce of courage and strength I can muster to finish with a personal best. A final heart rate of 144+ compared with a resting rate of 41 during taper week. A 16:10.009 wasn't good enough to place in the top 5, but the PB against the clock was my goal— Yay! Next time, sub-16!

This was my demonstration of staying in my lane, but only for swimming—and track. I knew completely that one day if I lived long enough, I would fulfill my truth—as I felt it even then. Living my destiny meant my lanes would change openly and abundantly—I did not know exactly how or when but trusted that someday that would be clear. In those days, I was my own coach working my body and mind together in a synchronous performance in the water—today is much more directed to my coaching of others, offering my help with His message to anyone challenged with their own transition or even the education offered to others how real this transition is—to everyone involved. When one rediscovers their truth and the message of reality it brings, 'staying in your lane' will no longer be the right response. To those who think it should be, I fondly offer this reply—*"Well, frankly Scarlett, ...!"*

A CAREER PATH BEGINS
WHERE SPORTS LEFT OFF

My [father] cautioned when I was entering college and looking for a major and minor to *"Keep your options open. Don't get too specialized in a career that will back you into a corner if things don't work out"*. And my immediate choice was to turn to an industrial specialty that I enjoyed teaching. Yes, at the time I was in the middle of a housing boom in the Midwest that drove my interest and my skills working with my hands and mind together. Building trades and manufacturing fascinated me and I wanted to be a part of it for years to come. So, taking a teaching certification path with an industrial specialty in those early years seemed like a responsible move that would pay dividends most of my life—and still be able to use my love of sports and helping others at the same time... and if at all possible, obtain a paycheck to at least keep pace with the bills.

With that in mind, I pursued a secondary teaching certificate with an industrial arts specialty focused on architectural, mechanical, and technical drafting. In those years, the course content was driven by mechanical equipment that was a glorified T square affixed to customized tables for skilled draft persons. I was particularly enthralled with a high school drafting class with whom the instructor was among the best I'd ever had direct me on a path that fulfilled a number of personal goals. Being involved with an industrial craft and being able to demonstrate a finished work of which I could take pride was quite gratifying and timely. Now it was appropriate to put that into motion for the springboard of my career.

After completing my three-year collegiate career with a 3.43 GPA and enough hours for a double major, I felt the need to start my working career seeking a teaching assignment out of state if that was possible. My search with the University placement program landed me at a Catholic school, a little bit out of my comfort zone but seemed like a good fit. I remained there for two years leading a one-person department before I was offered tenure—something most in the teaching profession only experience after at least five years of optimum performance, most in the profession strive for IF they intend to make this a long-term arrangement. I did not—that was not something I chose to pursue. Where they're offer was attractive, I found it extremely difficult on which to base a 12—month life on nine months of pay. Although customary in this profession, I didn't feel it was something well-suited over the long run. Where teaching itself was a valuable exercise and one I intended to continue in some way, this particular district and locale was not where I wanted to plant roots. But it is worth noting some of the experiences during my two-year run provided a substantial platform for the rest of my life.

Teaching at a Catholic secondary facility as a layperson had its advantages. But it was also a good learning experience acquainting me with a different religious perspective. Being raised in a Protestant family environment (and parents of a Mennonite and Penn Dutch heritage) through mostly attending confirmation classes and occasional holiday services, I was only marginally acquainted with the Catholic traditions. I was required to attend but not necessarily participate in weekly 'mass' services in the gymnasium. My role was simply to maintain order within my homeroom assigned class.

During my time there, I also took part in a memorable spiritual experience hosted on a weekend at the HS's governing Convent. Referred to as 'Teens Encounter Christ' (TEC), I took part in a three-day lock in that became one of the most moving and rewarding spiritual experiences I've had thus far. I left midday Sunday having made a valuable connection with people I never knew before this and I'll never forget after. Fascinating and certainly thought-provoking. It allowed me to openly challenge previous conceptions, and to throw away conventional thought and prejudice. At least for the weekend, I was able to bond with others on parts of their journey they were willing to share and learn from each other—one more way to learn from others as well.

Starting my teaching career focused on an underfunded, floundering department with marginal support and even less enrollment spelled potential doom for a subject destined for removal if something was not done well and soon. I began my assignment with a full load of classes each day ranging from freshman to advanced level drafting. The advanced courses were more directed at mechanical design, offering brainstorming sessions that helped expand students thought process into a very distinctive 'what if' perspective. They would be offered a scenario of an industrial setting and were asked to re-purpose a machine or manufacturing system to make it more relevant and easier to complete production output. Better said, given a business environment, students would be asked to redesign old systems to make more practical and useful offering whatever new ideas they could. That was the intent. For the two years running, the class made outstanding achievements and offered masterful ideas many of which have infiltrated today's manufacturing world (things like solutions around robotic automation, remote activation that keeps the worker out of danger, etc.). Some ideas were even entered into a local science fair which produced several awards and nominations. For a program nearing extinction, this was a major shot in the arm and notice to administration to retain it. And the kids loved it! Really pumped me up knowing I had a part in it. Enrollment and interest in the program began to skyrocket that next year.

Being largely a lab environment, my double-sized classroom held 35 students in each of five classes every day. That kind of environment allowed me much more one-on-one interaction getting to know my students far more individually than a lecture hall or traditional arrangement. My initial self-directed goal was to reach everyone in some positive way, even those that other teachers had limited hope over the years. It seemed like my courses were considered second class but drew many talented and skilled kids previously left untouched. It was my intent to do everything in my power to offer them insight and reveal those skills in a meaningful way they could take with them well beyond this classroom. In the two years I was there, the department enrollment grew 300% and was re-directed in a more technical view previously absent. Helping kids see things not staring them in front of their faces was a challenge I was easily up to.

However, I was not prepared to address an absence of basic math skills during my very first semester. My first course focus took two solid weeks to address math skills of fractions and decimal equivalents they were expected to use to measure on a scale. These were the days of manual computations without the benefit of computers, cell phones, much less doing a Google search. There was CAD (computer assisted drafting), but only in local trade college courses or industry applications. It was all I could do to buy vellum and mechanical pencils for the department on a $900 budget. But as I soon discovered, the work was worth its weight in gold.

The most moving point, among many during my time, was two months before graduation my second year. School administrators decided to have their yearbook signing ceremony four weeks before the end of the year allowing interaction between students and teachers before completion of that term. Where that omitted the graduation and prom ceremonies with photos as keepsakes, it did allow that exchange of signings and unique demonstrations of caring I had never experienced before. For instance, here are some highlights from their handwritten entries—

> *You have been my favorite teacher for the past two years and thank you for helping me out in drafting. I hope you do well at your new job. I think we will all miss you very much our senior year.*

You are one of the best teachers I have had. I decided I'm going into the field of drafting all because of you.

You're the best teacher I've ever had here and I'm forever grateful for getting me started in drafting. Good luck on your new job and continued success. Please stay the way you are now—one hell of a good person.

You are a heck of a teacher. Thanks for all you've done for me this year. I feel I learn more in this class than any other. You're a great teacher. I hope to be as good as you and drafting sometime.

This has been the best class I ever had. You weren't like a teacher to me, but more like a [brother]. I don't think this class will be the same without you.

I only knew you for two years, but it was the best two of my schooling. Stay in touch!

As startling as this was for me, it demonstrated how special these bonds can be and that I wanted to continue this path as the basis for my life's calling. And my coaching work at the same school added to that strong connection with a primary life direction.

Taking charge of the HS cross-country and track team of both male and female athletes was a welcome opportunity to work in my childhood passion and get a stipend for doing so. Where that money was minimal (amount and incentive), my zeal for helping kids excel in these sports materialized as one means of completing vicariously. Being fresh out of college and still in some reasonable shape, I became a 'co-runner' in which I openly challenged myself outwardly suggesting to the team *that "I won't ask you do anything I am not willing to try—assuming I can keep up with you!"* Establishing that credibility was quite important to me, given the fact that I was only four years older than the seniors on the team. I was on a 'first name' basis, also not widely accepted at this ultra-conservative era and employer.

This experience was particularly rewarding in many ways. Two key highlights drove my passion and love even deeper—

- Gifted runners come in all shapes, sizes, genders, and races. This team was blessed with more than three state-quality athletes on both boys and girl's teams worthy of current contention for state level competition. And a dozen more with far-reaching potential to do the same IF their passion withstood the conditioning and retained their self-drive to excel in their HS career.

- Simply stated—these kids rocked! Nothing made my work more enjoyable that being able to see kids succeed and achieve a personal best that is ONLY measurable in THEIR world. My role quickly moved to 'cheerleader' during their meets—quite the challenge on expanded cross-country routes where I ended up running their three-mile course several times to see as many runners at as many points as possible. That passion and love of the kids came natural to me—something no one could suppress.

The cross-country team had a relatively disturbing past. Their home course selected was a local State Park, extremely wooded to the point it required extreme skill and negotiation of the runners hurdling fallen trees and exposed root systems making tripping a very real hazard. I would have none of that. Where my decision was questioned from the top, my rationale stood fast. I negotiated with a nearby park district to use their beautiful grounds offering a flat terrain and open field of meadows. There was ample parking facility along with enough acreage to see runners across the entire grounds of their three-mile trek. The kids loved it! And that really was all that matters. Even opposing teams were thankful that someone made a choice to give them a safer race in which to compete.

And their uniforms sorely needed replacement. So how does one do that on this salary and no budget? You skip a few meals and bite the bullet. One weekend I paid a visit to a student's parents silk-screening shop nearby to select new team jerseys for all 11 of the starting runners of each boys and girl's cross-country teams. Made for sparse September paycheck, but well worth the renewed enthusiasm in their eyes. Priceless! I even ordered a coach's jacket in matching colors with embroidered letters of the HS name and mascot—I couldn't resist!

In my younger days, this experience was a critical stepping-stone in my career AND life path. Setting the stage early was a clear focus giving me a glimpse of how to leverage and find immense joy in connecting with people of all ages and diversity. This also helped develop my life commitment working to eliminate judgment and pre-conceptions in anyone. From day one, I saw everyone as inclusive and a contributing member of the classroom and team. This was not a learned behavior rather something instilled in my DNA. It defined who I am.

BRINGING MORE LIFE INTO MY LIFE

Make no mistake, pinnacle moments in my life are many—of pain and of joy, anticipation, and uncertainty, of love and some of resentment. But nothing compares to the peace of one heartbeat next to mine, connecting in a pattern of rhythmic pentameter matched only by a shallow but deliberate breathing. First a son, then 16 months later a daughter—each profoundly appearing in my life when my hope of leaving some lasting legacy really began to take hold. These were very early years in my self-awareness but gave immense purpose and direction by focusing attention on these precious gifts.

My daughter was only one week old but with a seeming metabolism and sleep pattern of a toddler. The intense happiness of that moment with her at one week old, lying on my chest filled my heart with the peace never quite experienced before. When one connects with another—parent and child—the bond is unquestionably a power beyond normal comprehension. I was incredibly happy being consumed in that moment. We had learned in a few more months that her progression was quite profound in speed and magnitude of learning. Within the 1st eight months, she began to show major signs of independent steps upright—yes, she was walking at 9 months albeit somewhat unstable, but very real.

And my son also demonstrated early signs of learning and acute awareness of his surroundings. His late-night feedings and changes where highlighted with a tour of the house with a cradle in my arms that allowed him to see in the same direction as I walked—he wanted to see what I saw.

Both children were my definition of perfection in so many ways. They were blessed with physical health at birth, although my son contracted salmonella poisoning from the daycare passed to 21 other children after admitting him at 6 weeks old. Unsure if this is largely the cause of IBS to this day, but nothing was ever clinically verified to connect the two. He has since grown to a 6' stature, easily 6" more than I.

My daughter began her life in the womb as a double egg—an anomaly that often occurs without episode or overt signs in many pregnancies. The pediatrician relayed some of these findings from the surgeon who had revealed a theory as to why she had progressed so quickly. Her embryo was actually an eventual absorption of two eggs in one. Double trouble? Maybe, all I know is that she was the perfect picture of health with future revelations yet to be discovered. My love would grow in concert with both children well into their young adulthood.

I've heard it said countless times and will testify to its truth. After one has children, you'll never get another completely restful night's sleep again. Each has demonstrated their own passion for similar causes, each well-focused on a career path packed with challenges that each are fully equipped to handle and come out victorious. But they also understand the depth of their search for their own truth, perhaps in connection with what they have learned from mine.

I am convinced of their love for their family and their focus on living their truth—with or without me in their day to day lives. They are exactly what this world needs—now and beyond. Godspeed!

REDISCOVERY — A REVELATION!

Among the most difficult years developing my persona amidst an environment that demanded a distinct role, the last decade of the 20th century also proved to be my own 'coming out' to myself. The series of critical revelations was about to overtake everything I had questioned throughout youth. I needed to build on these new life lessons. With computers all the rage and the internet in its infancy, my exploration found numerous sites most devoted to the subject but more in a focus of physical presentation than actual gender identity, or even the fluidity of gender across all humans.

My initial quest was abruptly stopped when I landed on one site that allowed users to create an opposite gender image when a photo is input. The site was accepting some custom adjustments for glasses, hair length and color, even some facial features providing a real transformation causing my surprise and amazement. This was <u>really</u> me, at least she certainly looked like me! Like a lifelong disguise had just been removed. That connection was not just coincidental or chance, this is what I had to see to believe—to begin to better understand now that everything experienced before was for a distinct reason.

This was another 'thump on the head'. Like art imitating life, everything happens for a reason and moments like this contribute to the climax of the story. This was exactly that!

Seeing several websites linked to this, there was one that particularly caught my eye, located in the near west suburbs of Chicago. I know the area well in my numerous business travels to the city but planned a trip to see for myself. With only one makeshift outfit assembled from Goodwill purchases, I stopped by 'Transformations' at one of their two shops late on a weekday evening after most traffic had subsided. After a short period of browsing several racks of clothing, I was asked if I would like to use a dressing room and undergo a makeover to which I agreed. The makeover came first. Meeting the proprietor, Rori, and her son Soto, was the beginning of a relationship best described as my founding Godmother. The outpouring of love they extend everyone who enters their shop is something to witness and learn. Their primary clientele is cancer patients with whom breast forms or other replacement alternatives are well adorned on their store shelves. Quite frankly, for me as one just beginning this chapter, it was like being a kid in a candy store. Where do I start? But she also gave the Trans community a safe place to explore and ask questions—a vital resource certainly for my journey and revelation.

I can only imagine the feeling of loss of a loved one that confronts anyone experiencing cancer. To that I can only relate the experience my sister went through before passing from stage four lung cancer and then my brother's prostate cancer surgery a few years later. And my best friend in Madison experienced a breast reduction from a suspect tumor several years ago from which I agreed to watch over her during recovery—that was the least I could do after she watched after me recovering from a 'rhino/septo' procedure in 2007—affectionately known as a 'nose job'. To date, I have been immensely fortunate to be free of such trauma.

With Soto completing my makeover, I proceeded to my dressing room, struggling to avoid smearing the artistry she just produced. Stepping out of the dressing room in full garb for the first time looking at a full-length mirror brought tears of joy and revelation to me and a sense of peace never experienced before. I composed my excitement and proceeded to pay for their services. A small price for what they just gave me. At check out, I was asked for my name and if I plan to return? *"Absolutely!"*, I replied. Then I began to give my name when Soto abruptly whispered *"Shhhh—What is your 'fem name?"* Without hesitation, Teri was born —a name that will become legal after two long decades but time necessary to build the confidence and self-acceptance. That was a big mountain to climb!

Why the chosen name? For the spontaneity required at that moment, all I could think of was a special female of whom gained so much of my affection and admiration during my high school years—Teri. She was undeniably one of those people I could never flush from my memory even as all these years had passed, and I never saw her beyond the three class reunions we traded brief histories. That part was easy… but the last name came almost as quickly serving as a place in my racing life as a 'miler' in both track and swimming. Seemed like 'Miles' was a sound choice. And so, it was written, it's stuck ever since.

Before returning to the hotel that evening, I accompanied the two of them to a CGS (Chicago Gender Society) function nearby serving a dinner and dance after. CGS was quite active in the community and Rori had already gained my trust, not an easy task. Upon our arrival at the dinner, it still amazes me to this day, we were greeted by a receptionist and coat check associate. We preceded to a ballroom where no less than 400 transgender men and women 'dressed as expressed' adorned the place. Hallelujah, I was not the only one and certainly <u>not</u> sick -something my father had labeled me years ago!

Following were several years of more discovery—searching for some physical validation—in some way to 'see' and feel the person before me, stretching to become more visible. In those early days, even now most times money is tight and any ability to find an outfit was subject to both having disposable income (which is still very sparse) and a means and place to store it. For me, the only place that was within my control most of the time was a small cardboard box under my desk at work—not something I would dare attempt today, and really was not a smart move then. But I had no other choice—for the mean-while. And that was about to change… Enter Laura.

After meeting my special friend Laura at a 2009 convention, her outpouring of kindness was certainly unexpected but equally timely and very welcome. She lived in a neighboring state, it was still a healthy drive that put at least a full day behind the wheel. Where that had its challenges, I was elated with her offer to store some things in her house. She had moved here several years ago from the East Coast bringing with her bride and her dentistry practice. Laura had lost her spouse to cancer several years ago and was now living alone in a relatively spacious home. With much of the basement unoccupied, she agreed to provide temporary residence of some of my belongings which had since exceeded their single cardboard box confinement—still necessary boundaries, but I could now expand—slightly. Clearly, the Trans-angels were looking over me. Laura to the rescue!

Shortly after, some business trips that took me close to the area provided an opportunity where I could relocate some of those clothes in a more hospitable setting. This unsurpassed friendship spawned a key reason, amongst others, that I decided this area would eventually be a suitable home for my future. Those other reasons include a powerful—albeit limited—momentum shift in the local Trans-movement for which there would be numerous other local events that gave my objectives even more credibility and assurance—THIS was where I needed to be! But there were many other unfulfilled challenges and discoveries yet to materialize...

HALLOWEEN FUN

Halloween was almost always a date on my calendar that I tried to plan around representing one of the biggest moments of coming to terms with my transition. This was a ceremonial time of year many in the Trans community found some solace when 'passing' was not an issue—at least not for one or two nights each year. Whatever you looked like, no one really noticed or cared.

Shortly after seeing 'me' for the first time in the mirror at Transformations, those Halloween festivities helped propel me to a new 'step' in finding my look. The critical difference with those along a similar path realized that this was perfect way of exploring a way to define their identity—that each of us were trying to darken up those shades of gray to fit comfortably in our own skin.

It was super fun to experiment with something for which there was no perfect answer and no one to judge you—it was all in good fun but exponentially important to many of those in transition especially at the beginning of their journey. What other time of the year was it completely acceptable to dress up as anyone in anyway and never be asked questions—and in many cases, completely open in some 'contests' if one chose to compete for best costume? Some were dressed in goth, some in renaissance, some in political figures, others in historic periods, and some who had among the most dramatic and realistic makeup that would rival Hollywood artistry. Fascinating... and I was in! Not so much for any competition, I was not into the showmanship. But I was keenly interested to learn more about how to dress (including what did and did not look good on me!). It was a great way to learn how to improve my makeup routine including contouring and shading, even some special techniques I still use today—airbrush (my primary tool of choice). But my favorite costume was my 'Queen of Hearts' where I even got brave enough to try some fake tattoos.

One year, Laura, Teri Jean (TJ), and I convened in Chicago for a Halloween celebration. The three of us took a limo ride—we all pitched in and rode from the hotel in the burbs to Boystown where we took part in some dancing at three separate places each until exhausted by midnight. After dinner at The Kit Kat Club and dancing at Sidetracks and Roscoes, our adrenalin was still pretty high and very welcome. The walk back to the limo pickup point was still several blocks away, but what a fantastic night seeing all the others out celebrating together. For me, I don't know that I had that much fun that late at night since college days. At least I was smart enough to bring a pair of ballet slippers to walk back to the limo from Boystown, otherwise my feet would definitely never let me do that again.

Since then, I have returned to the Kit Kat again for outstanding food with a Martini bar that is to die for. And if one is not careful, they are so tasty and so smooth it is really easy to overdo it without realizing the effects—one of the reasons I elect to do ride-sharing every time I revisit that area for dining and dancing. On one of those trips, I was fortunate to meet and share a drink and conversation with RuPaul where she was performing near the Kit Kat Club. She was so kind and open. Never realized her statuesque profile until in person—she towers beautifully over my head. Wow! For an old fart, I was really getting into this—I felt 21 again, at least for one night.

FINDING MY PRESENCE

My newest revelation at Transformations in the Chicago area was clearly a necessary jumpstart to my rediscovery. But none more important along the way than I want desperately to attend a church of acceptance—commonly referred to as O&A—'Open and Affirming'. I had not the best experiences in previous attempts and thought I would give this one more shot with the referral of some local friends I had met through Rori. They had invited me to their suburban church one Sunday, that became a major positive step in my affirmation and with their help. At first sight, this looked like 'Little House on the Prairie', resembling a country church built long ago and the city eventually grew up around them, but with a very warm acceptance and family feel. After years of being snubbed and shunned in countless other religious 'places of worship', the Trans community has been singled out as the most unwelcomed group in an otherwise God loving environment. The practice of Jesus's unconditional love is a traditional test that few hard-core religions can truly exemplify—but there are some and this was one last hope for me to continue pursuit. So, volunteering my own vulnerability did not come short-sighted or without substantial research and planning. But, certainly by first impressions, this place was clearly different—a feeling of grace and love permeated my soul when I entered the sanctuary. Their strong reputation of all-welcoming was most definitely fulfilled those first three years getting to know several members. The hardest part was leaving them after each service mid-week and some Sundays when my business commitments ended. But their impact on me was profound those early years—and still is. Each Sunday, I still try to attend their Zoom meeting services and sometimes their virtual coffee hour, depending on conflicting commitments and simulcast services of other local churches.

Just because a church calls itself 'Open and Affirming', does not automatically mean everyone there feels exactly that same way. That was a hard dose of reality I had to face in entering new spaces and houses of worship where often congregations faced many of the same issues dealing with culture change that meant a major paradigm shift. Many experiencing those 'houses of worship' in their early years of reaffirmation may have lost a significant portion of their original congregation members. Although some would have successfully replaced those with others now welcomed, that's an exceedingly difficult move to make—EVERYONE on this Titanic has to know what is in store if they don't adjust their course and EVERYONE has to take steps to avoid it… that often takes years to recoup losses amidst that redirection. The message for those with the desire to worship in a place who will TRULY accept everyone as they are? Do your homework, but don't expect miracles. Be prepared for setbacks but in most cases, the reward is well-worth the risk. It takes time and perseverance—this is probably the hardest culture to change—that of a religious setting or even your loved ones who may be at those same crossroads.

There were some who were clearly uncomfortable with my presence those first years of intermittent visits. And when my friends who had moved away, I remained, again only during those driving trips to the area. I was delighted to have reached a critical milestone, to be able to worship in my true identity—female. Without reservation and amongst those willing enough to see me through that surface, and because I had no instruction or understanding how to adjust my voice, I chose to say little at least until those first few years had passed. Perhaps odd, you may think, but still very necessary—to me. I took great pains to never breach the trust and acceptance by allowing that male persona to resurface in any way. That was never me. In those early days of transition, this was no easy task, still learning all phases of those transformation skills. A challenge to anyone's definition of courage and determination, often bordering on insanity trying to be all things to all people, exhausting to say the least—became a way of life for several more years yet. This was one of my earliest doses of reality that I would not keep this up for long. I couldn't!

Preceding one of my trips to the area, I contacted the pastor asking if they would have any interest in my leading a discussion with their adult bible study group regarding the transgender community and questions they may have during their 'outreach'. I know that my presence had always created angst in some people, certainly joy in others, and questions in everyone. I always admired the love they had for each other, clearly demonstrated in these types of meetings after service. I was always amazed at their candor, their desire to learn more and their ultimate sincerity. It was refreshing to see and experience. This made perfect sense since most of those whom I met seemed to want to reach out, but perhaps not really sure how and reluctant to try. I wanted to help them through that in some way. They agreed to schedule a time and I planned accordingly. I was absolutely awestruck by their offer and looked forward to meeting many friends again.

That Sunday when I arrived, I was greeted with a reception that seemed like what many families might experience when a soldier returns home. Where my arrival certainly can't compare with that, they definitely made me feel loved. To me, that's all that counts. After the service concluded we proceeded to the social hall for coffee, then to the classroom for our adult study. After a 60—minute meeting, each of the dozen church-goers had asked ample questions and even helped shed some tears with me. Telling one's story is never easy and even when requested, shows a vulnerable side that demands authenticity with courage—on both the teller and the listeners part. Apparently, I had demonstrated that characteristic in particular when one of the elders voiced his remarks in front of the group, *"Teri, you are an amazing lady with class and courage beyond compare. You have spoken from your heart and given us all reason to want to learn more. Thank you for coming and sharing your story and having patience with us all. We all love you!"* This came from a man that I had admired for years based on his steadfast commitment to his community and seemed more open to learning more now. But we never really spoke much before that. Now I look for him every time. I do not know if this experience was one that helped push him from ambivalence closer to advocacy, maybe I will never know. But then again, it doesn't really matter. His comments and his further friendship every time I return is a gift to me. I am grateful for the opportunity this church has given me to grow and to extend that outreach to their congregation. Time—another great equalizer.

During another trip to the Chicago area, I stayed at a bed and breakfast in one of the nearby western suburbs of the downtown loop. One of Transformations remaining stores was located just up the street a few blocks, so this made perfect sense to accommodate one evening's visit to see her before leaving that Friday. This particular lodging house was absolutely gorgeous in both vintage architecture and landscaping and well-adorned inside with all one could ask for in a very warm and 'homey' feeling.

After checking in with the proprietor, a very friendly widow, I explained my transition because of how I would present myself in fem regarding my plans for that evening and that the security camera may pick up a 'stranger' that hadn't been seen earlier. She explained that everything would be fine, and I should park in the back away from traffic and visibility. Although that struck me a bit odd, I proceeded with my plans dressing in full garb for my return from Transformations nearby shop. When I returned on that dark January evening, she had left the porch lights ablaze for me to negotiate the snow-covered walkway. But when I entered the back porch and proceeded into the main living space, the fireplace was beautifully inviting and warm, giving me a beautiful sense of comfort and peace… <u>until</u> I discovered that there was a kitchen and family room completely full of all twelve overnight guests staring directly at me as I walked across the room.   The proprietor had informed them that a 'Trans' woman was staying here and if they wanted to 'meet one', they could expect my return around 9PM and share some conversation. The reality of her offer materialized in what made me feel like I was the 'attraction' at the zoo—LITTLE conversation from anyone after *'Hi'*, but ample body language and gaping expressions put me into a very awkward moment—for which I confronted the proprietor the next morning at checkout informing her that I would be leaving early.

Even in my typical response to such situations in a passive resistance mode of those early days, I confronted the offender kindly and allowed her an opportunity to express her apology—everyone deserves that, enough to learn and reconcile such actions for hopefully changing future behaviors. I have not returned since but hope that she has used this as an opportunity to learn and know more about the Trans community. I believe her heart is in the right place. A win overall, albeit a painful experience for me—one of the many 'speed bumps' of this life. This was a definite learning moment for me, towards some sorely needed liberation and maturity.

GIRLS (OR BOYS?)

To begin at the end, let me leave no doubt that my gender identity and my sexual preferences match. Where some peripheral questions have surfaced since surgery, that still remains intact. But among my most profound adjustments is essentially a dichotomy—where my libido is a fraction of what pre-GRS male testosterone levels of 750.0 milligrams is now 2.0, my thoughts and attractions are still consistent and profoundly directed to those females bearing more brains and sincere smiles than purely chemistry (although that still counts a lot). What was once a pre-GRS feeling of almost daily release of sexual tension, there was certainly no sense of intimacy and little lasting memory of joy or satisfaction. But the other side of that coin is an increase in my own sexual and emotional awareness, not something I had bothered to study or really take the time or effort to better understand. In short, in a male persona, there were so many nuances of eroticism that were never really on my radar—nothing I took the time to understand or explore, certainly not without some research and toil. This was quite different and very new—and VERY welcome!

Much of my attraction from men was welcome, but only to the point of flattery, never something I would ever physically act on. I do, however, have outstandingly good and fulfilling platonic relationships with a few men, but never on a sexual level.

Other early indicators include my youth experiences in which I never had a lasting friendship with a male—not something I consciously avoided but was an undeniable trend. I did have one close relationship during my high school and college years who later disavowed me when I came out to him in 2009. I have documented high school and grade school yearbook entries all by females would also always describe me as a "good listener and advisor with deep sensitivity"—perhaps a good way of saying they were not interested? Either way, my female relationships and experiences were widely varied and never boring, to me anyway, but always very brief and never sexually tested. Perhaps that is why they ended too soon… I was a virgin until summer of '76 after starting a college semester late, end up getting my BS degree in three years. My focus was in and out, so my social interactions were few, especially living off-campus to save money. It was that summer of '76 when my girlfriend at the time—a cheerleader of all things—decided our preferred spot to copulate was at the same park at 11:00 PM on a Saturday night. And this is where I discovered chiggers, an obvious remnant of that foreplay for the next several weeks. Quite the telltale signature of foreplay and hard to dispute.

But among my key takeaways from this experience and most of the others, brief or extended, was my constant desire not to only be with females, but also to be them. Yes, this was a pinnacle revelation for me… the feelings that dominated these relationships was a need to be among females and as female. Again, enormously powerful underling themes, ALL very real! This was certainly one of the fundamental reasons that my interest was much less about sex and more about gender identity.

Conversely to all of this was one of about a dozen meetings, or perhaps better said 'interludes' with men in the early 2000s before surgery. One occurrence happened at a bar awaiting our table for dinner reservations when I was out with a lady friend in Chicago during a business trip to the area. Fully dressed in a business 'suit' (skirt, top, heels, and jacket), I sat with her next to each other sharing a few drinks and great conversation, even though I was very attracted to her and she to me. But we both noticed one elderly and rather good-looking man gazing at me in something more than a casual glance. He found his way over to our table and asked if he could buy me a drink, then proceeded to touch my exposed knee with plans to explore higher, I am certain. My abrupt response was to stand from my stool as poised as I could and to calmly inform him to, *"Remove your hand, or I will!"* We left immediately—my first of several related experiences.

A similar experience occurred in a neighboring Chicago suburb, also pre surgery experience after visiting Transformations, getting dressed and meeting a friend of hers at the local neighborhood lounge. After dining on their scrumptious, seared tuna steak, we met her friend at the bar where we both seated next to each other. Clearly, this male friend was well past major drunk, proceeded to tell me how I had to *"…help him release his pent-up sexual energy!"* because he thought he would 'explode' from just looking at me sitting there. Really? Honestly, is this what things have come to? Where every girl likes a good dose of flattery, this was not it. I have been there, and I don't want to be the recipient of this kind of treatment. Enough! No one deserves that. I will not apologize for who I am. I demand the same respect and courtesy afforded anyone else. I stood glaring at him directly in those foggy eyes exclaiming *"Seriously? You have to be kidding me... never in a million years. It's just you and your hand tonight, Honey!"*, clearly informing him of my disgust and clarifying my anger with *"You couldn't keep up with me anyway!"* ... then promptly left the lounge in disgust. Rori quickly followed to apologize for his behavior. Flattering, hardly. Disgusting, absolutely! But each of these encounters gave me one more good reason why I chose to pursue a black belt in Taekwondo. And hoping I'll never need it.

This portion of the journey was not without its physical changes and increased sense of 'awareness' within my own skin. Where sexual sensitivity is clearly not the same pre-GRS, the sense of enjoyment is much more fulfilling, longer lasting, far more satisfying and much more intense. But it also requires a learning process—one focused on rediscovering who I AM and exploring ways I had never considered before. This learning is fun! And I say all of this to put things into a very purposeful message—NONE of this life [in relentless pursuit of my truth] has ever been motivated by a fraction having to do with perversion or sex in any form. Humans require love, and intimacy of some sort at some point—that is a fundamental need. I suppose one of the crosses I bear in this life must deal with continuing pursuit of that elusive blessing that helps define our human race. My last such episode sharing intimacy was when conceiving my daughter in 1991. You do the math. And for those who call this 'a choice' suggest you exercise those math skills pondering these facts and statistics. For starters, since 2010, I have-

- Lost two families, my home and house, and my most of my life as I once knew it.

- Spent over $35,000 on uninsured medical expenses, hormone therapy, electrolysis preparation, clinical psychology requirements, and untold out of pocket costs contributing to this transition.

- Post Op medical expenses, most associated with typical evaluations common to cis-gender females— although my definition of menopause is much different now.

- Undergone numerous instances of humiliation & shunning by those once called friends, family members or acquaintances.

- Well over $12,000 spent on moving expenses to find a new start.

- Over $770,000 of nearly a decade of spousal support.

The upside from all these expenses and trauma? Am I happy? Undeniably! I am elated with the new rediscovery of this truth that has eluded me for so many years. But contrary to what many friends have told me *"Now you can do what you've always wanted"* really do not understand. This is not a choice, no more than any other form of physical surgery or treatment—perhaps not as imminent as emergency medical treatments for life support, but it cannot be ignored and put on the shelf, or something others may choose to deny. It has nothing to do with what I want, but everything to do with being who I have always been. I will <u>not</u> hide in plain sight anymore! And I will <u>not</u> apologize for who I am.

As one could expect, especially fully invested in puberty, at this time of my growth and exploration led to some interesting relationships dating HS ladies or with whom I trained on the summer swim team. But in not one of these relationships has ever been a question to my sexual preference. And because I lost my 'virginity' in my second year of college, none of my HS or collegiate relationships largely ever involved much more than holding hands or 'making out'. Fast forward to present day, my current hormone therapy has stimulated instances where my only answer to that question (Is my preference still the same?) and yes, it is—that has never changed. Always ladies!

Although my statistics and figures are not typical, the amounts may differ, but the categories are often quite similar. Most such stories can give you much more in terms of lost dignity and the fight for basic respect that comes so rarely, and some even of violent or life-ending acts of hatred. And there are statistics that demonstrate how so many politicians and societies would rather just erase us from their reality we apparently threaten. Each year, global murders of transgender persons are recognized, mostly in private vigils across the world recognizing these tragedies, which never make it to the local news channel when 'celebrated' every November 20th. And even fewer are investigated by police or prosecutors to help end this violence. Trans women of color continue to lead the number of those murdered in our community—although none can be considered 'safe'. In 2020 alone, the US experienced an all-time high murder count of 47 Trans people and 386 world-wide—recognized in the annual vigil held each November 20th to celebrate those who were daring enough to live their truth. The event referred to as TDoR (Transgender Day of Remembrance) honors those who died between October 1, 2019 and September 30, 2020—all from the hands of violence which don't include the numbers of other incidents that go unreported and uninvestigated. We are NOT disposable! All [we] want is to be treated like everyone else—with the dignity and respect due anyone anywhere anytime. Nothing more!

CONVENTIONS AND CONFERENCES

E arly one summer, I attended my first national conference/convention celebrating the Trans community, each one on a related journey but all focused on sharing their stories and learning more about the community [and about themselves]. A Chicago-based event for four days was my first such gathering of so many people in search of answers to questions of their own celebration. This was a remarkable combination of people from of all walks of life, countries, cultures, and faiths all with the common theme of learning without judging. This was a safe space where attendees could feel comfortable in their own skin without the constant judgement outside the Convention Center walls.

There was so much to learn and so many people to meet, but only 3.5 days in full. I thought I was in heaven! So many opportunities—I was going to make the best of it and get substantially OUT of my comfort zone. Whereas some chose to use their opportunity as a chance to freely express themselves in dress, mannerisms, whatever they chose to identify was completely acceptable and encouraged during the week's social activities and workshops. But I was also extremely new to exposure at this level and still had my guard up—again, this comes with the territory. Having a safe space like this in the company of friends and meeting new acquaintances was a Trans person's definition of paradise. And I was in the thickest of it for the first time in my journey.

One sweet lady stopped and asked me for some help when it came time for her to return to her home in Tennessee. She had been saving for the last year to come up with the necessary registration fee and fell short on transportation expenses essentially hitching a ride with a stranger—a very risky move traveling fully dressed in partial transition exposed to public scrutiny. Some would agree that it was an amazing feat to just arrive here at all, completely safe and unscathed. But she still had to make it back home. A number of us took up a collection to make up the difference to buy her a bus ticket by the end of the week. To me, that was the first demonstration of unity and camaraderie to such an extreme level in folks who had only this one thing in common... but enough to bond and connect with some friends who have lasted ever since. Wow, I was in some gracious company! And many who came from all over the US, even some from Canada and Mexico, were shown kindness and sincere openness. Their offer of friendship was extraordinary, something I've not experienced most of my life.

In 2009, I met three of my best friends in the Trans community at this conference, albeit one of them in a rather awkward way. At least that's how I saw it. But she taught me immediately what friendship is all about and how to reach out. Before that experience I could probably have best described myself as socially inept not to mention uncomfortable in these kinds of situations.

During the opening workshop, I walked in and took a seat in the front row since no one else had occupied the room at the moment besides the instructor. The session was scheduled to start in five minutes, and I made myself at home. After scrounging around in my purse to locate a writing utensil, I noticed someone sit down next to me. My initial thought was *"Seriously? There's a thousand seats empty in this room and you find it necessary to sit right beside me?"* She immediately started up a conversation and my hard-nosed attitude softened immediately. Why not? Isn't that why I was here? *Quit being so darn stodgy!*

After a quick dose of hard self-coaching, we hit it off rather well and spent a large part of the rest of the conference recruiting others of a similar stodgy nature, softening them up and making friends. What a concept! Teri had just met Laura! I learned something incredibly special from this lady, how to be lovable and loving. We met two others that week who became special bonds beyond this conference. What a revelation! The three of us have stayed steadfast friends the last decade at first demonstrated when two of us went to California to visit the third during her GRS procedure. That alone tends to illustrate how these powerful meetings and friendships start out and progress.

A major highlight of the week centered around a special ceremony honoring those Trans veterans serving in the military each sharing their story of how they hid their nonconformity but continue to serve our country, a stark difference since the 2016 decision to discharge all current Trans persons and will prohibit future enlistments—for now etched in my memory was during the second year I attended, this time as a session host is serving a short presentation titled *"Details, Details; You Do Need to Sweat the Small Stuff."* The focus was to address some fundamental mannerisms, dress, voice, gate and even some discussions about makeup and hair. After attending last year's session to learn for myself many of these topics, I wanted to share more with those searching for some advice in an open forum discussion that promoted free exchange and interaction. 21 attended, but all gave excellent evaluations and were engaged in open conversation sharing their learnings and ideas and I was asked to return for next year's convention. I was completely amazed at the level of sincerity an authenticity displayed by those attending asking perhaps the most elementary questions, but truly something they needed some insight to progress in their journey. This was an epiphany for me realizing the immense impact this had on so many. Wonderful! A living testament that everyone is on a different path on their journey-something to respect, to learn, and to admire.

I SHOULD NOT BE HERE!

High school and grade school gym classes were some of the most difficult times growing up. Not because I was awkward at sports, rather at feeling drastically uncomfortable in a male locker room. I had no business being in there. I knew it was wrong as a child and young adult and in later years I made a conscious effort to dress and shower at home after workouts at local fitness centers. As inconvenient as this was, it was necessary. Even using the toilets was only exercised in an emergency. When a local fitness center opened within a mile of my current home, this made things much more reliable planning methodically how I would arrive & leave without entering or using anything but the actual equipment and floor areas of the main gym.

Of even greater discomfort was when I had to use the 'facilities' when working at the office or hosting a training class—when I planned my bathroom use during hours or locations far away from frequent access by others. This was a daily routine that was among one of the biggest reasons for my request to work from home on a permanent basis—something the Covid-19 outbreak has given ample justification to resume until retirement. Perhaps one of the only good things from Covid!?

Several years passed before I moved forward in my transition and my self-realization that this was not something one can put on the shelf—or walk away from in denial. Even those of my friends who have undergone the dangerous life-altering effects of conversion therapy will tell you that this is a part of them that can NEVER be pushed under or denied of that truth that will haunt them forever, despite other's agenda. I can't begin to recap those years, even in college, where I tried with all my power to be the male, I thought others wanted me to be, but with no success. Attempts at emulating my brother at his fixation on weightlifting seemed like a means to 'look the part' as much as I could muster. There was a point shortly after college where my upper arms grew to the same size as my neck—all simply because I thought I was supposed to. And to my surprise, no one noticed or cared—and I was so ashamed of myself and of burying my truth. To this day, I have no vivid memory of those days nor of my physique—mostly because I shredded all the known photos of those times in complete embarrassment of myself and my internal weakness allowing this to take over. This was NOT me! Not now, not ever!

I long for the day, soon, where I can be in the bathroom in sync with my revised gender (and locker room) without shame or discomfort—the one I belong in. Soon… VERY soon! This also means being able to resume swimming for conditioning—maybe someday to compete again, but only if those with whom I compete will allow it. For that, the jury is still out!

Even more important is my dream to return to the water

someday to workout in much the same body I was born with although some necessary 'adjustments' several years ago to bring everything into perspective. I recall making my debut in a lady's water polo team tank-suit a few years ago for the first time since surgery. Sitting on the side of the pool almost put me in a trance… staring at my feet dangling in the water realizing that these were the same legs that put me on the map in 1972, and again in the Senior Games in Palo Alto 36 years later. The hormones and surgical changes had sapped my strength to near zero, but nothing could dampen my love for the water and constant dream of one day returning.

Even if I'm not allowed to compete, I would still like to take part in some way or offer my help coaching. The change in gender had nothing to do with my technique, my knowledge and skill or my zeal. My age may have something to say about that, but time will tell—so far, so good!

Shortly after the turn of the 21st century began my quest for a new hobby, that would exercise my body in an individual manner like the way the water and the pavement or open countryside have become my sources of contemplation. Kayaking on the open river had its certain challenges, among which included the strong upstream current and the rocks and partially submerged fallen trees that demanded constant attention and numerous portage points.

I could explore the outdoors at a time when frozen waters were running clear and the 'state bird' had not yet arrived [the mosquito]. And my connection with nature was the experience I had long anticipated—seeing the shoreline teaming with skunk, deer, woodchuck, and beaver… and the majestic eagles flying overhead... absolutely profound timing to witness first-hand nature waking up.

But my quest, to meet myself on a completely unfamiliar platform challenged me in a new way—to connect with nature and talk with my God. Putting the boat in the water at dawn paddling upstream as far and fast as I could prove to be quite the workout. But seeing the sunrise and drinking it all in gave me was well worth the work. I was able to move into a new world, self-challenged, and begin more to exercise my changing identity as much as I could. Great therapy for body, mind, and soul.

SENIOR GAMES

In early 2008, I received a notice announcing a senior level meet in my state that would lead to a national competition if I qualified. There were two separate qualifying meets I had to achieve minimum time standards—one for track events and one for swimming. It had been 15 years since I competed casually and almost 35 seriously. But it seemed like the right thing to do at the time filling a void that was becoming overwhelming. This seemed like the perfect diversion or temporary substitute once again, from living exactly as intended. Since I was still hiding my true identity, I competed in the male events in both venues and qualifying in each. If I made the minimum time standards, I was destined to compete in Palo Alto, CA in August of 2009. Since family members had earlier decided against attending the state qualifying meets, I should not have expected any different reply when I contacted them about the results. *"I made it! I can't believe it! We have a date in the Bay area next summer—the whole family can go!"*, to which the returned response came *"That's more than a year away. We'll see what is scheduled."* Rejection and disappointment were commonplace, so this really wasn't unanticipated. But the pain was still a constant reminder. It was never brought up again.

My training increased considerably those next 12 months, both in the pool and the track. Although the training distances and interval conditioning were nothing compared with collegiate levels, it was enough for the race as I had qualified to swim and run. When August arrived, I was more than ready and super excited just to be a part of it. When I arrived in California, I was prepared for the two-week stay since swimming events were on the front end and track on the back. I was able to meet some amazing people who had traveled from all over the country to come to this one place to compete and reunite with old friends. I don't recall ever seeing so much spandex and 'skin suits' in one place before! And the overall climate of everyone competing and attending seemed allot like a collegiate meet. [I was back home!]

The Avery Aquatic Center at Stanford University is among the most state-of-the-art natatoriums in the US. Our events were to be held in the 25-yard pool while the 50-meter pool was being used for water polo tournaments. The bulkhead was placed near our competitive lanes separate from the deep end where warmups were allowed during events. I prefer competing in long course events to reduce the number of turns but that was not going to happen at this meet. Besides, my events were 50 and 100 yd. freestyle. My qualifying times put me in the fast heat for each pitting me against some of the fastest in my age group in the country, perhaps in the world. But being in lanes six and eight was exactly what I wanted. I don't want center lanes because I don't choose to pattern my performance against other swimmers rather against the clock. This usually requires intense discipline but became my preference long ago. In the 100 free event, that worked well placing 5th overall.

The 50 was slightly different. Being an immensely challenging sprint event, I often say it's the only race swum 'before you hit the water'. It was clear that other participants were deep in their own zone working through the race in their mind as a customary preparation. But I had been through this so many times before and was competing here for two primary reasons-

- To prove to myself I could still do it after all these years and had the wherewithal to endure the conditioning required.

- To have fun, meet as many people as possible, and recall this moment when I return next as 'female' (IF they let me).

I was in the far lane, well-away from the fastest swimmers for the 50 free. When the gun went off, I was nearly first in the water making major headway into the turn bringing the wake with me—exactly the plan—to help carry me away on the final lap. Hitting the turns with precision of appropriate timing and speed can't be more critical than now. But I had not anticipated the affect from the sun's position from the change in the time of day. Where that would not have any exposure with an indoor pool, in the early afternoon the sun cast a shadow on the bulkhead that created an illusion I had not anticipated in warmups three hours earlier. Misjudging that distance from the wall, thinking I was close enough to flip, I missed! OMG! I had to frantically wave my arms to push me backwards enough to touch the wall and push again, but by now it was too late. I ended up 5th in this heat and 11th overall, but still with a near personal best time. And I was NOT disqualified. Lesson learned—although distance events require much more conditioning, they are vastly preferred and always leave you room to screw up and still correct [most of] those errors.

During one event I watched as I waited for my second event to begin, I witnessed a female swimmer (age 95) complete the two-lap event in a record time for her age group. Where the actual time is not material, the standing ovation she received once she finished was something to see in person. Even the announcer over the loudspeaker said "Let her be an inspiration to those in the stands. Let's see everyone out here in two years competing again!"

The track event was hosted near the end of the games. Probably a good thing because I was pretty spent from warmups and the excitement at the Aquatic Center. Now I was competing in the half mile event, again incredibly competitive and required high placement or low times in 8 separate heats of the semi-finals. I was in heat #6 putting me still in strong contention but needing a great performance to qualify for the finals tomorrow. Only problem—I had a return flight home in the morning, so there were no plans to stick around for those even if I qualified. My objectives were exceeded! I won my half mile heat in a personal best at age 55 (2:21.90), but probably not enough to have qualified for the finals anyway.

At least that is what I thought until I received the final results that next week indicating that I had—but I was obviously a 'no-show' heading home. I had done what I came to do. I recall messaging my kids about the results getting a return text of 'Congratulations'! That was my <u>real</u> gift.

REBIRTH—
THE DAY OF ALL DAYS!

My GRS experience was, to say the least, a pinnacle event giving me a rebirth unmatched by any other in my first six decades. The morning of the scheduled procedure on October 10, 2016 it was raining and storming, but not inside me! I recall being at immense peace—in a trance most of the night before. The surgeon picked me up at the rehab center where I would spend the next 4 to 12 days in recovery. I was on my way!

With little sleep the night before, Monday's alarm came none too soon, in typical fashion. I awoke 90 minutes before my scheduled departure. My pre-surgery preparation was performed at the surgeon's office after he and his assistant picked me up at the hotel to drive to the hospital and office. My head and heart were remarkably solemn and content, not in fear or unrest, not even overly excited. I know of stories of others who got cold feet and used this as an opportunity to back out or reconsider what they were about to do. Or at least a major discernment about losing what 'part' [they] had grown accustomed for so many years.

But my reflection was none of that. I was at peace. I was on a mission since birth, to be reborn and re-emerge as true self, one suppressed for so long in so many ways. Trust in my God was never more profound or apparent to me. He knew exactly what He was doing, including the trials and trauma I needed to endure to get to this pinnacle moment. My vitals and shower completed the prep, and I was placed on the gurney followed by the anesthetist. I attempted counting backwards from 1—100 left off at #78 when I said to the nurse, "*I think you know the rest, I'm going away for a little bit now, thank you.*" An after 4 1/2 hours in surgery I was now in recovery for another two, then whisked off to a private room for the next three days. I know that Anne was with me during those moments as she had promised—to see me before entry and upon moving to recovery. I don't know that I have seen a better sight in my life since my kids' birth—Anne's bright smile welcoming me to a new world in a new (revealed) persona.

On Tuesday following, I recall being stirred by the nurse checking on the IV and my vitals. When my head cleared enough to fully grasp the rebirth and the gravity of what I had just experienced, tears erupted in a flood. A new child was born and a new destiny to fulfill the way I was intended. No remorse, no regrets, nothing missed, all welcomed, all at peace—a peace unlike anything that has come to me, like a waterfall! I was so filled with immense peace with knowing one of the major pieces of my puzzle was now complete.

During my initial episode lying there in my surgery recovery mode, I was completely vulnerable and yet filled with faith and comfort. I felt almost weightless, in assurance that I was exactly as planned. In my turmoil grasping my new reality, I apparently triggered the nurse alarm without knowing it. When the nurse came in to check on my stitches, she exclaimed *"Wow! He does good work!"* My physical change had moved more profoundly into my psyche and my heart.

The next two weeks was spent in recovery gaining enough strength to make the 12-hour drive back. Having Anne with me, she was still able to work on her computer for those 7 days with me, and still managed to look in on me constantly. And with several stitches trying to separate, the risk of tearing more was very real. Being very intentional and diligently careful of that next week, was of particular concern and focus. I was immensely thankful of Anne's magical touch. After the procedure and following 5 days, Anne was called back home, but not before Laura made the drive all the way to Philly to provide the next five days of care and the subsequent drive home. Both Angels demonstrated their friendship and their commitment to supporting the Trans community in a massively important way. There was no way this life changing procedure and rehab could be accomplished successfully without them. For that, I honor them with my constant and unconditional love.

I was able to proceed home with Laura by day 12 then followed by six weeks of supine position on the couch where I could work on my laptop even on camera. as is said in many business settings and in Hollywood, *"Never let them see you sweat!"* I was even able to host team meetings and webinars from my new 'office' layout.

I was able to return to my current church community shortly before Christmas but still unable to sit comfortably.

This was a slow healing process that was partially complicated by three daily dilation exercises required for at least the next 9 to 12 months. This was necessary primarily to avoid necrosis that could essentially nullify the surgery goal. The exercises, although very necessary to stretch tissue and muscles, were never tested like this before, served to work against the struggling healing of the herniated stitches. A real dichotomy! This was the part of transition that tends to drive one crazy waiting for the body to adjust in a way it has never been asked to do before. But the cause, need and mission would not be stopped. Patience and courage were called upon more times before just like this. Just stay the course!

And true to form, by early summer 2017, my post-op return to the surgeon was exemplary, per his words. Dilation would continue for life, but eventually tapering to twice a week. Sensory feelings return about 90% by early 2018, a renewal was well underway! But one of the most pronounced changes although I still struggle at times is the pride that I carry knowing my complete transformation is one major step closer to fulfillment. The preceding 23 years has left me with a passive response mentality that conceals my emotions, reactions, and tears. I have promised myself that this practice will cease and begin I shall carry this transformation in my walk, my speech and my love expressed far more openly and fluently. I will not be held back anymore!

A NEW BEGINNING: MOVING ON SOUTH

Working for a large fortune 100 company has some benefits. Actually, several! For nearly 23 years I have come to realize both the ups and the downs of corporate life. But also, within a corporate culture that demands conformity often leaving little personal choices. Coming out at work was never really an option although I did manage to inform three people over the course of my tenure. My closest teammates would never have tolerated this, and their responses would vary from applause to outright hatred. The diversity of potential reactions was evident in daily correspondence among which one instance between team members consoled each other when discussing the local school district challenge of allowing Trans students in bathrooms of their gender identity. One responded with *"If I had kids, I would never let them attend that school if they allowed it "*. And as that burden increased over the years, unless I could answer this question to myself with a positive response [What is to be gained by telling this person?], I chose to remain silent. Perhaps the easy way out but understanding your audience and their capacity to adapt, accept and understand change is an essential charge each of us needs to weigh before divulging your truth -coming out to anyone. My survival instinct was more important than my exposure.

In 2012 after spending a year living in a distant Chicago suburb, I asked my new manager if I could live anywhere else—a place where I could afford the cost of living and housing, and where the general political climate was more aligned with mine. This area rapidly had become too costly with too many bad memories at a time in my life I needed to seriously look at planting some roots. After looking over dozens of neighborhoods and over 65 houses in a three-day trip to the area, I landed in a community that had many advantages and minimal drawbacks. But the good outweighed the less than good. After almost eight years I am happy to call this home.

Since moving to my present home in late summer 2013, most of my neighbors have been less than neighborly, something I suppose is another indication of how divided this country really is—but I remain hopeful and optimistic that things will improve over time. When I first moved in, I decided to exercise my welcoming strategies learned in church earlier last year. I patronized the local grocery store to locate some mouthwatering pastries worthy of gifts to my neighbors. I selected one each of apple, cherry, and pumpkin pie for neighbors on each side and in front of me. My first neighbor to the west spent little time at home and was appreciative of the gesture, but that was among two of the remaining times we spoke, mostly because of his work demands in a neighboring state. The other neighbor on the east side was less responsive and said thank you, but that was the last I heard of them for the next two years. Occasionally they would acknowledge me when shoveling their drive in the winter or raking their leaves in the fall. Much the same reaction from my neighbors across the street. The occupants of two of the three neighbors changed in the next six months. The family to the east remains the same.

My western neighbor was soon replaced with a newlywed couple when I first met them. They were trying to start a family and having difficulty on their own, so they elected to adopt. Within six months after that adoption took hold, they conceived a daughter (of course—instant family!). I was quick to inform them during my pie welcoming gesture that I was in transition and they might tend to see two different people working outside around my house from time to time. No intent to alert me because I'm the same person. I don't think they really grasped the situation or clearly understood, nor did it necessarily matter to them—at least not overtly. It was this family whom I later discovered about their struggle tolerating what they deemed 'my lifestyle' that bordered on their definition of 'religious love'. I clearly did not meet their standards of living or being, simply trying to be myself was not going to be tolerated well. Perhaps that's why they elected to move—I don't know. Shortly after that exchange I saw a for sale sign in their yard. Before the movers came and they had to relinquish their property, the husband managed to say to me *"We love you and will miss you. The kids adore you and made you this card themselves. Thanks for being our neighbor."* Maybe there was a spark of hope from serving as an example of loving patience helping someone without that understanding—to open their hearts AND look deeper than their current mind-set—in short, to question their current values and philosophies that may need some adjustment. I believe a seed was planted, that hopefully, someday will take root and offer a substantial means of reflection and eventual alliance. We both deserve that chance!

The eastern neighbor does not grasp my transition as I relayed that to them the same way as the western neighbor. They have chosen to avoid making eye contact with me. This even after my welcome gesture shortly after moving in. Not sure they really understood my message but did not stop me from proceeding to other neighbors. I guess this is their defini-tion of being neighborly. I won't expect much in the future but remain patient with those open to learning.

In mid-summer 2018 the 'religious' family to the west had moved on and was replaced with a new owner. I suppose the new owner had been here much sooner as our paths did not cross until I noticed her mowing her yard one day and stopped over to welcome just as I had the others but this time without a pie. Her massive ear to ear smile and offered handshake was so refreshing —and that coupled with her greeting made my home seem much more secure and happy. *"You probably noticed"*, she said, *"I'm a lesbian."* To which I promptly replied, *"No not really… should I?"* After I threw down my guard, I offered *"Well you probably noticed I'm Trans!"* The connection was sponta-neous and instant but equally profound, and a friendship was born. Knowing that a real live neighbor has your back is worth gold. Seems like my move has begun to reap some rewards building on a stronger and resilient support group is priceless!

MY FAITH JOURNEY RENEWED

A new church where I would be myself was high on my list of critical things to do having just moved to my new 'hometown'. This church was absolutely breathtaking, clad inside with ornate stained-glass stories of biblical events and wonderfully wood-crafted vaulted ceilings, stage, pulpit, and pews all magnificently maintained from its birth 150 years before. Beautiful is an understatement, but unmatched by the welcoming extended that morning pretty consistent through the next four years. And to my surprise, a distinct part of my initial impression was marked by The Prodigal Sunz, a local quintet who played magnificent inspirational and spiritual gospel music in an acapella format—a priceless way to greet my 'new' church. Fabulous! I knew I was in the right place at the right time.

In typical form, I quickly offered help. I became a self-designated dishwasher for the next few weeks, not minding a bit, getting involved up to my elbows was absolutely fine with me. I was elated to belong somewhere. Kitchen help quickly morphed into a monthly workday—one Saturday morning a month in which the church members would volunteer to help with landscaping, trimming, housekeeping, painting, and general upkeep of the beautiful but aging building. I came to love this day and felt deeply committed to showing up every time I was able to accommodate the schedule. But over-extending that offer is also an example of a life lesson I have never seemed to learn very well. At least something that has helped my emotional and spiritual maturity. But that has taken a lifetime to better understand that process and my tendency to throw caution to the wind, assuming that everyone is playing within the same rules, philosophies, and expectations.

During many of the Sunday services, there were some hymns that just spoke to me or perhaps better said screamed at me (e.g., *I will Come to You*). It was He who called me to this place, and I was never more certain at the time. And more than once I felt the distinct presence of my sister and my mom sitting on each shoulder making certain I understood that this was the exact place I needed to be at this exact moment. I know each of them sat right there beside me, hands outstretched waiting for mine. There was never a doubt from the moment I left my northern-most home that THIS was where I was destined.

Each following Sunday for the next few years I've found my place generally seated comfortably in the center of the sanctuary sometimes with nearby neighbors, but I often sat alone. Where I did not take that personally at first, it became much more apparent especially during the later years. For the next 2 years, I experienced an outreach from Pastor Barb's leadership (the interim church leader before a full-time search was complete) of the Trans community and allowed me to help in that charge.

It was because of her direct involvement that helped bring the 'T' more in line with the remaining LGBTQ+'s of which the church mission—at least in concept. Since 2013 when I began, I remained one of only two Trans persons—the other who has since moved away from the area. Barb was instrumental in extending the outreach to a local Trans support non-profit agency bringing them into a physical space in the building that also helped foster the 'open and affirming' welcome mission of the congregation.

Walking through the church parking lot one Saturday following a 'workday', I recall being approached by a homeless man, Jimmy, asking me for anything I could offer him on a particularly brisk day. I promised to bring him blankets and a down jacket that next morning during services.

Although this experience was not new to other church-goers, it certainly was to me. That one-on-one dialogue with someone experiencing despair and near hopelessness of life on the streets cast a spotlight that morning directly on me and Jimmy. For me, it was the first of several confrontations with the realities of today's communities—not just in this city and not just exclusively affecting only one race or gender. But it was one key highlight that only strengthened my resolve to step up, get involved, improving conditions for the homeless LGBTQ community.

WHO IS LEELAH ALCORN?

Standing in a school parking lot in a cold rain pouring down just after the Christmas holiday had passed was not my idea of winter frolic, this now marking my second year in the area. In my world, snow is the type of precipitation you could bank on from late October to Mother's Day, but this was a cold that chilled to the bone. And the primary reason I was here was to mourn the loss of a local high school girl who had just taken her own life the night before—walking in front of a passing semi, a stone's throw from her home, at least the place where she had been sequestered in her room for revealing her truth at school. Although I know very few people since moving here 18 months before, I felt a calling to pay homage to stand with my community calling for change, to be sure Leelah's life was not in vain and was something deserving of celebration. Her courage was something to elevate, to emulate for the betterment of us all. Standing in the pouring rain was only one small way to celebrate Leelah's life. There were multiple such vigils across the globe for the next two months and was the ignition for a Trans movement that has only gained momentum since. To be a part of that event

—I am convinced God used in all of us attending to bear witness and give an account of what happened that night. Over a 3-hour candlelight vigil, amidst the pouring rain, no less than half a dozen Trans persons came out that night onstage announcing their truth as only they could, all in Leelah's tribute. More than one local TV station was doing a live remote asking for numerous interviews and commentary including one from me. And although I felt honored to give my perspective, I held nothing back including ample tears to follow. This was a moment like no other and I wanted to acknowledge very clearly the love and respect demonstrated that night was truly characteristic of every Trans person and every support agency I have encountered since.

As the evening progressed, Leelah's friends and many other anonymous people gave their remarks honoring her, it came over me like a sudden wave of emotion and with a spiritual connection I could not deny—a revelation that shook my soul to the core. Leelah's life ended in a traumatic way that must be the catalyst for us to stimulate change in whatever capacity we can—we have to act! I often feel sad for those who never take the chance to exercise the courage it takes to reflect on one's inner identity and to find and live that truth that so many others never seek and never find. We love you Leelah!

Here is an excerpt of a 2018 highlight of some sobering statistics from HRC (Human Rights Campaign)—

> In 2018, various Trans support agencies tracked at
> least 26 violent deaths of Transgender [or gender

non-conforming people] in the U.S., most of whom were Black women. These victims were killed by acquaintances, partners, and strangers, some of whom have been arrested and charged, most others have yet to be identified. Some of these cases involve clear anti-Transgender bias. In others, the victim's Transgender status may have put them at risk in other ways, such as forcing them into unemployment, poverty, homelessness and/or survival sex work. [1] Every year there are more and more violent incidents against the Trans community most of which go unreported and uninvestigated. This violence has no basis for causation, no provocation, and no place in society. They are perhaps best classified as hate crimes—purely out of malice.

Leelah's death was completely unnecessary but certainly was the only alternative she felt was something within her control. Her life was taken from her from and we each share an obligation to emulate her message and continue the momentum she started.

Each year the Trans community and their advocates mourn the loss of those whose lives were removed from their control, violently murdered for no other crime than being themselves. Celebrated in a vigil format around the globe, November 20th signifies TDoR (Transgender Day of Remembrance) this memorial each Thanksgiving season giving us another opportunity to regain that momentum and begin to chip away at lowering these statistics.

To lift a critical summary from HRC, they have positioned this best, articulating exactly the context of this global problem and what we must do to find resolution-

> Since 2013, more than 130 Transgender and gender-expansive individuals have been killed in the United States. Even in the face of this physical danger, hatred, and discrimination, Transgender Americans live courageously and overcome unjust barriers in all corners of our country. But until we as a country collectively address and dismantle these barriers, Transgender people will continue to face higher rates of discrimination, poverty, homelessness, and violence. While it's tempting and common to pursue largely reactive and temporary solutions, we must address the root causes of this violence to make our communities safer for everyone. It is unacceptable that Transgender and gender-expansive people are killed simply because of who they are. It's not enough to grieve the loss of victims of anti-Transgender violence. We must honor their memories with action.[2]

There is never a basis or justification for any hate crimes in this world, absolutely none! To defeat hate, we need your help!

GETTING MORE INVOLVED

It seemed like the time was right for me to commit even more to this church. But I was still exploring those opportunities and sorting some things out. There was a series of events getting involved, immersing myself to get that sense of community. This will help demonstrate my spiritual connections in those early years and the life lessons along that way.

Among the things that interested me most was a book club that seemed intriguing. It was something that seemed a win/win in several ways, among which included a demonstration of my outreach to improve a renewed sense of belonging and getting to know others far deeper than simply saying 'Hi' on Sunday. This was a source of new perspectives and education. Some to a fault! I was involved in reading some of great interest and fascination and others that, quite honestly, bored me to death. Each month, different members offered their homes to host the group for the 'book of the month', followed (of course) with a loaded buffet of various cuisine and wine. This part was new to me, still learning to cook and entertain others, to keep up with the Joneses of the church—it really wasn't a competition because I was clearly outmatched. It was all I could do to feed myself, although I have improved over time. And on a very tight budget, this became a definite but very welcome challenge. I was in!

In a June meeting, we were discussing a book I had recommended, Princes Warrior, the story of Kristen Beck, a 36-tour Navy SEAL who was also 'male to female' (M2F) transgender. But she had not come out until those tours were complete. A very moving tale—that was also the source of one book-club member's reaction who began to challenge the discussion with some personal questions directed my way. One of those questions changed my demeanor, and apparently an outward expression when asked about "*...my choice of bathrooms that did not seem appropriate...*" Being a member of an 'open and affirming' congregation who now challenged that label and my dignity, completely put me at odds. I tried my best to remain poised and contained. But true to form, at least this time in my journey, when such challenges present themselves, I tend to clam up and say little else—at least until such time when I can think things through and process hidden meanings more precisely.

Perhaps that passive response comes from my history of past relationships of loveless parenting and marital relationship, and self-absorbed employers were constant reminders of one's 'place' and who was in charge. The message of my parents and marriage have been established earlier, but I also had my share of managers where some would even say *"If it wasn't for me, you wouldn't have a job".* Therein lies one of my dominate challenges throughout life in a daily balance of humility and confidence without judging others but remaining firm and convicted in one's guiding principles—a fundamental tenant demonstrating grace in every possible situation and relationship. Having a backbone with sensitivity and tact!

The best manager I ever had reminded me regularly why she hired me, *"I didn't hire you to agree with me, I hired you to challenge me and teach me. That's how we all get better!"* Improving my character is my ultimate goal! When she retired two years after she hired me, I recall approaching problems and relationships in the workplace with 'What would Linda do?' She helped me craft a presentation for one of our larger customers demonstrating the value of servant leadership all in the context of Jesus teachings. And where many may follow a different perspective or religion (or prefer none at all), few can dispute the positive impact of a leader who recognizes everyone as a contributing source of progress—especially when they practice humility with unconditional love—a rare breed!

The next day when I saw these people again at Sunday service, where the host of Friday's book club stopped me in the narthex and asked if I was OK. He had noticed my abrupt changes in expression and dialogue following that comment at book club, it was an undeniable reaction I could not disguise. When I explained my plan to leave the church-at least for the summer, he quickly followed with *"Don't! Please stay! People here love you. But you need to understand that everyone is on their own journey, not just you. Give them time and give them your love. You won't regret it."* That point hit home—one I still practice today.

On one Sunday after service, I ran into the book club member who asked that question earlier at our meeting. We spoke at length about her comment. She apologized for any misunderstanding, and clearly, she was sincere demonstrating a loving response that was welcome and well timed. Later, she was the same beautiful lady who welcomed me back in the sanctuary the first Sunday after my two-month recovery exclaiming *"Wow! You look amazing! How are you feeling? We are so happy to see you back here with us!"*

As one of those monumental moments, this was going to be a big one! I participated in more and more book club meetings, as much as I could keep up given an increasingly demanding work and travel schedule. Some of my work demands would take me out of state for weeks at a time with the territory that spanned coast to coast. In a coaching and support role for our field staff, I was typically in pretty big demand as well as that of our customers. I tried to schedule some of those commitments around church functions. I wanted to reciprocate the kindness extended by so many, so I volunteered to host the first book club of the New Year following Christmas celebrations. When scheduling conflicts surfaced, the move to February was agreed for me to host the group. In my haste, I had forgotten that their customary monthly meetings were held the 1st Friday of each month. OMG! That was my birthday—the big 6-0! When a few others called that to my attention, it was too late to back out now. Again, I was in!

Planning for book club was far less a challenge, but I had no idea how to plan for a birthday. As it turned out, I did not have to. When 30 people arrived, my relatively small and humble house was packed SRO! We shared buffet items so that all of us prepared a mini potluck, followed by traditional and abundant cake and ice cream topped off with 'after dinner' Malbec. Wow! Clearly, this group knew how to cook, to eat, and to party! This was an evening the likes of which I have never experienced before. Wine, side dishes, salads, hors d'orves of every sort lined my humble basement table—the extended Thanksgiving table my father had made from Cherry years earlier—one of the few intact pieces I inherited from that place where I grew up. It was lined with dishes of every sort and heaped with mouth-watering samples of the cooking prowess these people were known for... an absolutely astounding delight for everyone. I think that was the evening I even had my first taste of raw mushrooms and lived to talk about it.

> [Sidebar—I totally detest mushrooms in all forms, especially sauteed. When my mother would sauté them on an open pan in the kitchen, the smell drove me absolutely bonkers flooding the house with the aroma some may call it—I call it a 'stench', stopping me short of outright gagging. This is my kryptonite!]

Every guest who came to the book club also brought a card placed in a small basket on my kitchen counter. But I was spent... emotionally drained and exhausted from prep all day and hosting until around 11:30 when the last guests departed. Generally, my body clock begins to shut down around 8PM since my rise time is at 4AM typically reserved for weekday workouts before the crowds gather at the local fitness center. My mind and heart could have gone all night, but my body said, *"No way!"* I left the best of the evening to give my attention that next morning. Little did I realize the impact of those gifts left that evening before, that would set the tone for the next year.

That morning of February 6th, 2016, my journey had officially entered a 7th decade. This new decade would help define the previous six. And it seemed like a short night of sleep since my normal weekday rise time is engrained in me all seven days a week. But Saturdays were meant to catch up on sleep, somehow. Fixing a hearty skillet of Jambalaya seemed appealing and a good way to use the produce that may otherwise go bad before a week of business travel. Noting the pile of unread and unopened birthday cards from the night before seemed like a good diversion from a sense of routine, but not before a fresh cup of coffee (yes, even on weekends). One by one, each card was carefully evaluated as to greeting, giver, and message… which was not a quick task. I quickly became absorbed in the activity, but never did I anticipate what was about to happen.

As a child, that time waiting to open presents on Christmas morning was one of those things I often thought of my parents loved to see their kids squirm and fidget with that anticipation having one present opened at a time in a round-robin typically covering three to four hours. Depression-era parents save everything, even wrapping paper from gifts year to year.

The exercise of opening these cards were full of that child-like excitement simply from each source's profound message. None were brief at all! Each had either the entire blank space filled with text and some covering the entire front and back where there was room. And a select few had inserts that continued on a separate piece of paper. Each word meticulously handwritten with immense support and love articulated in their own way one can only describe as a collection of love letters to me —not in an intimate sense, rather completely welcome as spiritual and personal. Again, in typical 'Teri' fashion, my tears streamed profusely covering my torso even sending me into what I can only describe as what one may experience from a nervous breakdown. Sobbing, to the point of convulsions lasting only a few minutes, but enough to send me to my knees experiencing nothing like that in two families—nothing has ever been close. Upon regaining a sense of composure, I realized that three hours had passed to absorb the impact of over 30 cards. Truly this was a gift never known before with a profound effect on me now, my support to proceed in pursuit of a planned medical revision was now firmly established—put the wheels in motion!

JUNE IS PRIDE MONTH

Before 2015, I had never attended or participated in this annual event. The Chicago parade was the only one I had any familiarity. And exposure to that one was based only on testimonies from local Trans and LGBTQ+ communities and news footage from local remotes. This new area was quite different as I soon discovered and after returning from a long stretch of business trips, I was ripe for more exploration and outreach. In 2014, I had turned down a request to organize and lead the float and parade primarily because of my limited outreach since moving here so recently. I would prefer learning more first before leading—something I practice in my work experience to build on things that work well and offer improvement advice only after learning the facts up front. I witnessed too many times in the business world, the arrogance of those who think they have all the answers without knowing the whole story first. Where the offer was a bit flattering, I was not ready. Others may see new blood as a great opportunity to avoid previous commitments and place on new unsuspecting contributors—but I took this as an opportunity to provide needed input. These people were different! *"Thank you for the offer, but I would prefer to learn more about the event before taking this on—but really, thank you for thinking of me!",* I responded. For once, I was thinking clearer. But I did commit as a marching member in this parade and the next few before Covid-19 hit in 2020. The events were fabulous displays celebrating all factions and walks of life, something none of my previous families would ever understand or tolerate, which in a sense, made these much more liberating experiences.

Two of the next three Junes, I was asked to deliver a testimonial on a portion of my story. I thought that this would be a real opportunity for the church to demonstrate how it gave any attention to the Trans community. Where it did allow a temporary glimpse into a fraction of my Trans story, it became more transparent that I seemed to be the only source or rationale for that display. And as much as I openly admitted on more than one occasion, I did not want their mission to be about me, I wanted to challenge them to live their vision and practice what they preached. As these first years of my experience were progressing, it was becoming clearer to me that being 'Open and Affirming' was really only true when any Trans person willingly attends service without being asked. But that only happened once in the six years I was attending—the active outreach to the Trans community seemed to be missing—at least from my vantage point. There was evidence of some outreach in the sense that other tenants within their building or leasing space as support agencies to the LGBTQ+ community. One of those groups made it a point of openly avoiding a connection with a religious space. But there was still a strong verbal message of welcoming and acceptance from church leaders and in the congregation.

Because the Trans community has been traditionally so maligned an overtly shunned, few have gained or been offered the trust of any religious institution. From conversion therapy to complete exclusion, the animosity has grown to outright hatred from some factions. For me personally as a Trans-person and church member, it became progressively clearer that my journey was really more of a novelty—something of a Hawthorne effect once my surgical changes were complete. There seemed to be nothing more that others felt was worth talking to me about or looking any deeper in what I had to offer—or who I really was in my heart and soul. When surgery was complete, so was the journey —and the support(?)

One Christmas I was asked to be a part of a skit that was apparently something that was done as a holiday tradition of sorts. This involved me posing for a reading in the church's 'Tonka Toy' Christmas, a reenactment of a Trans girl's child-hood struggle when given a traditional toy truck to play with as her parents were devoid of what internal challenge she was trying to sort out. I agreed because it seemed like a good way to at least give some attention, albeit brief, to the subject of one Trans journey. But over the next few years, there seemed to be less interest in exploring more or reaching out to any-one in the community. Pretty much 'one and done'. I recall one church elder openly sharing their views about a concern that outsiders would not attend if they thought it was a gay church. Apparently, a bad thing (?). Perhaps my presence here was not [as] welcome as it once seemed. [Has this train left the station! Maybe my time had run out and I had run my course.]

The journey of others evolves and changes, just like mine. That reality was staring me in the face over the next three years where I experienced more withdrawal of that support following my surgery. Since moving here, my friends were mostly composed of church members and some from local Trans support groups. My next-door neighbor's demeanor and attitude really did not change—they were still not very neighborly at all; perhaps that is just my particular neighborhood, but I am not sure they really are anywhere.

On the upside, some very encouraging experiences were becoming more available for which I had to take advantage. Getting involved in my own emotional well-being was not something I paid much attention to in past years. Among the local favorites became my attendance at a local symphony. Considered a formal affair by many, normally a little black dress event to which I dine out before and attend alone. Where I would love a companion, it has become way too much of a task laden with uncertainty with near constant disappointment.

Many refer to my OCD as unnecessary structure and planning. I prefer to think of it as very necessary offering a form of respect and decency. I do not venture in places unknown without considerable research knowing the dangers that I may face from others who do not want my presence or 'my kind'. It has become a great way to re-discover myself in a more liberated and comfortable way without the overt judgment and scrutiny of those who don't value my friendship or company.

Most places I go alone, but with much planning—concerts, restaurants, wine tastings, sports events, shopping, church… everything. This is where my OCD kicks in, big time. I have reluctantly come to terms with that reality having grown exhausted of being rejected or stood up—perhaps that is a characteristic that comes with the territory, or perhaps I just expect too much. Countless times I have extended offers to others, often met with indifference, noncommittal, or even completely ignoring me. When someone blows me off or forgets me completely after making a commitment, I do not tolerate that very well—again, a character flaw in me? But those whom I call close friends share a deep respect for common courtesy—of treating others just as [you] would want to be treated. It really isn't hard.

If you hadn't figured it out yet, among my key flaws is my 'anal' side of planning such things as outings to a fault, attempting to locate venues traveling with a secure feeling in parking, walking, and attending any event or activity. Where spontaneity may make one more 'fun', it often is not a practical option when one is in transition—that is a survival instinct that comes with this territory. Consider this 'Gal's Guide' that includes research and planning to account for such things like-

- Site proximity to restaurants and decent parking accommodations. Some parking garages are good, some not so good. Lighting and layout have everything to do with how secure someone can feel. Would be assailants can hide in many places and can easily be overlooked by most of us. Be alert at all times!

- As much as I love my heels, it's always smart to walk to public venues in flats carrying the dress shoes in

a bag. And depending on your dress and venue, that may help dictate what you have on your feet, carry a set of tennies or ballet slippers.

- When possible, make a point to tour the area as a preview of parking proximity to surrounding merchants, other vehicles an even distance from home. Know where you're going before you go.

- Price ridesharing services to see if availability and timing might be a good option.

- Text a friend or neighbor about your plans and timing of anticipated departure in return. Always have an ICE contact in your cell phone directory—In Case of Emergency.

- Verify the weather forecast to be sure you are ready for any extended walking or stoppage if your car gets stuck or compromised. This may mean snow or rain demanding boots and/ or an umbrella.

- Keep any relevant identification and/or letters from your surgeon or therapist if you have not yet undergone a legal name change.

- Do not forget to keep current license and registration in your auto glovebox including insurance verification.

- Although a bit pricey, AAA is a Godsend! Remember, where insurance covers the car, AAA covers you—the driver.

- On more than one occasion, I have met some 'ladies' in a pseudo—Trans role in which they openly pretend

to 'pass' as female to the Trans community, but
not so open to the men they prefer to tease when
trying to hook up at the bar scene. This is not only
a dangerous move to everyone involved, but it also
paints a horrible picture to real Trans persons who
are in a true transition mode in their journey, that
adds to intolerance, and worse yet, may stimulate a
justification of hate crimes of violence… NEVER a
good outcome and NEVER a smart thing to do.

There are many who refer to me as a Girl Scout, others as
OCD—probably best a blend of both as I gain more familiarity
with places and outings, this list grows a bit shorter but never
far from priorities, especially when exploring new horizons.

A GREATER SENSE OF PURPOSE

On more than one occasion, four to be exact, I was hoping to connect with people in an incredibly helpful and meaningful way—something so that a real connection would make a substantial difference. Putting things in perspective, much of my previous life was spent for someone else's definition of importance or value having little to do with my specific talents, skills. Certainly, nothing aspiring to what I defined is a necessary mission. Purpose was everything at this point! To me, the previous decades were mostly played out in fulfillment of tasks and situations that largely were someone else's design and focus—again, the experiences helped form who I am and have become. For that I am eternally grateful. Where my affinity for individual sports provided a significant series of character-building exercises, giving me a life of direction (at the time), it remains the primary reason that dominated so much for so long. It had to! It was my plan for survival but also a rule that would ultimately have little to do with my truth.

After losing my sister in 2012 and my mom two years later, that wake-up alarm loomed large ever since and has only contributed more to that drive -to do something that will leave a legacy serving many especially those less fortunate and those with whom I share a common bond. My mission was to establish a foundation in this city (and hopefully with a spreading outreach well beyond) earmarked for homeless Trans persons, a largely forgotten statistic with no real means of structured or sustainable support.

Where there are few bona-fide statistics or data to support my mission, that also is very common. Most such situations are borne from real testimonies from those struggling in their home life with families who 'did not sign up for this' —the revelation from a spouse or adult coming out with that announcement. Some are being forced to continue to live at 'home' in a sequestered room or some means of living out their truth still in a largely hidden way. Others opting or forced directly to the streets may also find themselves ostracized at their job—or outright fired for being who they are and 'disrupting the workplace'. And the trauma to a family's children cannot be overstated, certainly the younger they are, they tend to be somewhat more transparent to them from what they experience in their later years. But ALL of it comes with a price, and each with a message that will not make the papers, or the news media contribute the data that reliable agencies will deem credible. Data drives action, but ours often does not exist.

Through significant research and volunteer work for which local support agencies tend to focus their attention less on the Trans population, and even fewer addressing adults many of whom have lost everything to the streets —a growing concern of a population in receipt of critically limited resources for help. And when forced to turn mainstream services, many are met with resistance for much the same reason they were forced to the streets in the first place by simply how they identify and present themselves. Leaving little choice to survive, those who do often turn to drugs, sex trades, even theft and succumb to violence is all too common across this country.

But I understand at least enough to realize that such a foundation to succeed and be sustainable, must be built on character as well as money. Gaining more insight in local missions helps give me a greater sense of purpose and will contribute to what someday will aspire to that supporting foundation of hope. But where and how to start? The church was my early source then, providing ample opportunities to offer help. Volunteering gave me that personal drive seeking a very new perspective.

Volunteering is exactly that; putting yourself out there to serve and support, demonstrating love and grace in every situation. All with a focus on a purpose much bigger than yourself, expecting nothing in return. That focus became my entire sense of why I am here, something confirmed one Sunday morning at our adult study group preceding weekly church service. The topic of study this particular day involved homeless of the inner city and began to focus on LGBTQ+'s in the neighborhood. A guest speaker was leading the discussion from a nearby youth home specifically for serving that population of LGBTQ+'s, most of them there from injustices and shunning experienced from family or friends or disappearing support for those now forced to fend for themselves on the streets. That was where I first focused my attention and my contributions—quickly becoming my priority of service. I was very purposeful asking for church support but wisely expecting none. This was not something I wanted to force others to prioritize but they were very welcome to join me if they chose to. I helped lead food service and donation drives and move this agency to a list of benevolence giving which I offered to match that amount for a Christmas gift. This part of my support to a local mission lasted about two to three years when a HUD funding grant put them in a place where they no longer needed us—but something else did. I was invited by this group to be a part of a special focus group with another church member for a startup support agency that would provide foster care to those transitioning from the youth home for up to a year's stay or longer term depending on need. Our role would be to help with developing criteria for host home parents providing a loving environment for Trans clients. I underwent complete training provided by the agency and security clearance so that this role also prepared me as a coach and liaison offering guidance to the parents when questions or concerns surfaced. This provided a connection of service also exposing my vulnerabilities but facing them openly and without hesitation.

On my first assignment, it could best be summed up as my last connection resulting on my self-removal, at least in part. Where I was making distinct progress with a homeless 'Q' person, my soft heart got the best of me and I abandoned my training. Breaking some cardinal rules, especially on the first assignment is unforgivable. Not once, but three times. Do not give money (twice) and do not give rides (once).

Mine was supposed to be a position of coaching, not dona-
tions. Much like I learned from books and experience, this
was an essential life-learning building block necessary in this
constantly evolving, complex world.

Number three attempt at offering help was among the
most hurtful and potentially damaging experiences of my
new life since moving just after a few years ago. After witnessing my mom's last moments, overseen by a visiting nurse
appointed through her insurance plan for Hospice care, I was
close enough to see what type of care and passion the nurse
had for her job and her clients. And when attending a church
adult study session about hospice care, I quickly volunteered
to enter a training program for the neighboring state's local
caregiver certification program. After four weeks of instruction and exams, I was awarded a test assignment at a local
nursing home for the memory care unit. I suppose that was
just to get my supervisor a review of how I performed on my
feet with direct client interaction. Of particular importance
here is to highlight my preparation for most all of this. Up
to this moment, this was a key piece to the puzzle. Including
my final exam from the training program, I had purposely
presented male simply to gauge their acceptance of Trans
persons. I knew a complete security and background check
would be performed as a key part of this, which I passed
without flaw or hesitation, again all in my current legal name
and persona. My focus was to be in the role of caregiver to
the 11th hour LGBTQ+'s in their last days with no one else
beside them. I was painstakingly careful to share most everything about my journey and how I wanted to support those

in need just like my mom experienced. This was a crucial element to my decision to even proceed at all after my opening meeting at the hospice care office. I strategically and clearly informed my supervisor and the entire caregiving team about my GRS plans and timing and how I would present this day forward. With the affirmation verbally given to me the first day, again true to form, I was all in! Those remaining five meetings in person were all as I presented in my true form and dress today, again completely 'accepted' by my supervisor and the dozen caregivers on the team... or so I thought! I took great pain and effort to be honest, authentic, and transparent as possible.

Sunday, I proceeded to my appointment to visit with the same (ALS) client at the nursing home the previous week. I arrived around 12:30 as one would presume, she had no memory of my visit last week. After checking in at the nurse station I met her in the central living space where numerous other clients and some family members congregate. We spoke together, soft, sweet, tender but happy. We took a short stroll in the courtyard talking all the time and basking in the sunshine. Her smile said it all. She stole my heart for that short time, and after 45 minutes had passed, I pushed her wheelchair back to the living room space, said goodbye and checked out with the nurse. All was good... then!

That following Monday was one of my normal office days where I made the 14-mile trek to my then assigned office space. We had moved to a larger office setting in 2014, now housing over 1700 employees from four different companies under one enterprise. My little cubical, my temporary home away from home, was tucked away in an area void of most human life but occasionally inquiring ears were never far away. That made this day particularly uncomfortable knowing my ability to conceal my truth this public (my only remaining reason for retaining any portion of a man's wardrobe), was easily compromised given the phone call now coming in. It was my 'supervisor' at the hospice care headquarters with whom I had given this number only as an emergency source, my cell as the primary choice. That one did not ring nor was it ever tried.

"We have a problem", she opened with immediately. *"We've had a complaint about you and feel that this may not the place for you."* When I promptly asked *"Why?"* and *"From whom?",* all that was offered was *"From the client's husband, the lady you saw in the memory unit in the nursing home yesterday. He was sitting in the same common area where you were talking with her and demanded that you never return!"* It was clear to me about both husband and supervisor motives that I was being fired for being myself, something neither was capable of processing nor supporting. But why the sudden change now?

I was devastated! There I sat in my office trying to be as discreet as possible, disguising my voice from those overhearing and still trying to remain somewhat poised in the presence of such degrading news. How on earth can this happen? I was as forthright as I know how giving everything I had, laying myself out there in complete transparency and vulnerability. I knew the risk, but I was willing to take it based on the assurance I got from my supervisor and the team I would be a contributing member. How could they turn on me like this? I was appalled, angry, defeated and all those words wrapped up into one … but most of all, once again, alone. Feeling the tears stream down my face was becoming way too common. I had to find a way to harden up and to realize this was part of that journey I had to withstand to be able to help others with theirs. This was one more clear case of my character and my resolve. I hope I passed! Because this was Strike 3!

But I wasn't done yet! Without skipping a beat or missing a step, my quest for volunteering made another attempt. This time, again after meeting some special people at a church adult study meeting, one participant asked me to help the local homeless shelter for women of domestic abuse. She was reaching out asking for any help extending that outreach to the Trans community, a rising statistic in the intercity homeless population. After I was unsuccessful connecting through three separate exchanges in email, voicemail, and broken appointments at lunch and two outright no-shows, my patience ended, and I ran dry on future attempts. The last was a lunch meeting we both agreed to after Sunday church service when I received a text 15 minutes after our planned time that she had been involved in a car accident, discovered later from a church friend (a business associate of hers) that this was all fabricated. She was not in an accident and apparently had used this on other people. Seriously? People do that? Strike 4!

In 2018, another church member suggested that I work with a prominent Trans male pastor with local ties to our church in their ambassador program. This plan was designed to offer help and education through coaching and mentoring those congregations with an interest in learning more about LGBTQ+'s in their faith journey. THIS sounded like a compelling opportunity to learn, to reach out, and contribute in a meaningful way—and supporting the Trans community in that process. Completing an arduous and contemplative application process required significant self-reflection. And they required a self-made video as a bio to share with the other dozen on this group of applicants. But this put me at odds now—I had asked the pastor (the plan director) if there was a better way to correspond. I was not a Facebook user having way too much visibility of those whom I still did not trust still having much to lose if outed at work or online. He apparently understood suggesting I write my bio and send to the group on an email. An excellent idea, but short lived. I prepared a three-page bio on PDF and answered the fundamental questions posed to each applicant. I sent the email to all 12 and the director. But again, silence. Zero replies and zero communication to me after that.

I thought maybe it was me?! I reluctantly opened a Facebook account choosing to be essentially anonymous but was more open on email to this team. Again, asking the director for help and about his promise to host meetings on Zoom or correspondence by email, my response from him was ignored. After two more attempts by phone and email asking for some discussion about it, I stopped!

Teaching an old horse like me makes some new tricks difficult, so it seems. Through experiences like this, I need to take more ownership of things I can control and not of those things I can't. My takeaways from this include things to weigh carefully...

- Avoid assuming ill intent. Where it is a common response to return fire with fire, this is not always the case, and usually misunderstandings involve the offending party who simply did not know better. Of no malice, simply lack of education and foresight. Happens to ALL of us, some more than others. Being watchful of other's responses AND your reactions are equally critical parts to a successful outcome and an equation that can spell 'understanding' among all affected parties. Be loving!

- Don't be intimidated by someone else's agenda if it doesn't fit with your mission and your character but still be humble and willing to stretch yourself to learn new experiences. That makes you vulnerable. THAT makes you authentic!

- Recognize when personal shortcomings need work. My character struggles with being ignored and others who don't take responsibility for their own actions. That can be hard to deal with if you're not prepared to absorb some of that shock. Taking my own medicine is a daily requirement.

- Do not be compromised. Trust your heart!

Clearly, this road was never meant to be easy, even painful as it has been since my move in 2013. Tears have become less frequent, but probably more intense when they do happen. I still find myself awakening with a wet pillow realizing I had been in some form of pain that I could not describe to this date. But very real, nonetheless.

Topping the list of most of those early episodes would easily be blamed on hormones and with more accurately listening and centering. I suppose my reputation became painfully obvious to many at the church as a crybaby. Well deserved, maybe, but also very genuine!

THE TRIFECTA

A short two years later, a difficult year was brewing, but not until near the end. My sister had passed-away in January 2012 after a sudden and quite unexpected diagnosis of stage four lung cancer near thanksgiving. She had never smoked and lead a nearly perfect healthy life. No one saw this coming. At the family Thanksgiving dinner, she was her jovial, sometimes prankster self, but with reports of shortness of breath at times. After retiring earlier that June and passing her 60th birthday in October, all signs pointed to a smooth future spending quality time with friends, family, and local church functions. But this new health concern had other plans. By early December, she was on oxygen and the diagnosis was confirmed. A week later pneumonia set in so chemotherapy could not begin until that cleared up. Two weeks after that although pneumonia had subsided, cancer was in full tilt creating such weakness in her we could only wait, pray, console, and weep.

At the time, from my Chicagoland home, I was within easy reach to visit and stay with family for a difficult time. I recall moments with her as she sat in a chair with her head resting on a pillow on a TV tray, the only way she could breathe but still could not eat. When she struggled to ask me to gently massage her legs and feet to stimulate blood flow, I could sense a distinct presence of peace. She was content in receiving counsel in a spiritual connection that was very profound for each of us. The bond at that moment was perhaps the key moment when my sister and my truth met in spirit. On January 13th, when my sister left us, clearly a most trying time for everyone, most of all from the pain she had to endure those last hours. I have been truly blessed in my life in several ways having had very few such close encounters with the death of loved ones. This was the first so close to home. I don't recall ever spending this number of tears and sorrow.

Another pain point was that her final moment of life ended precisely at 11:58 PM on Thursday, January 12th, 2012, our mother's 87th birthday. No parent ever wants to see the day when they must bury their children. Her grief was tremendous and clearly, to her remaining family, was enough to consume her life for the next two years, what became essentially her preparation to be with her daughter. To that end, all financial commitments and family obligations were managed and completed. She was ready to join her daughter on December 22nd, 2013.

My mother was a saint to many, probably most profoundly to her children knowing the endurance she had to display on a daily basis within the marriage she experienced. Her relationship with her husband was one I saw progressively deteriorate all my life spent under the same roof. Where some may conclude that she was passively involved and avoided parenting where it was a necessary part of being a mother, we children discovered more about the constant stress she was under within his temper, his withholding of love for his children, all to survive. That was not fully understood until she began her new life on her own seeking an uncontested divorce early in the 1990's. Seeing her explore friendships with other relationships she had put on hold for years, it was so gratifying to see her smile, even travel with friends and family in ways she could never dare to dream when she was married. She was free to live herself, albeit alone, for the last 25 years of her life. And I was fortunate to see many of those changes.

I recall that early morning of the 22nd like it was yesterday. After receiving a frantic call from my brother about 10:00 AM on the 21st, I jumped in the car arriving around 2:00 PM just in time to see my oldest sister who had just spent the last 14 days at her bedside. Clearly, she was exhausted by the stress and constant care for our mother who was now nearly incoherent. After the Hospice nurse arrived at 9:00 PM and my sister left for her bedroom, I agreed to take shifts after sending the nurse back home at midnight. I took the first shift lying next to my mom's side, holding her hand, and talking to her. As much as I so desperately wanted her to know who her child really was, I thought better of it withholding that information again. This was not something I wanted her to take to her grave. My tears ran profusely and steadily for the next hour, only delayed by a quick bio break to compose myself. When I returned, I stepped up to the door threshold, looked at her expression and knew she had left us—she was gone. Again, my tears fell freely but now for both happiness and joy for her journey was complete and she was free. And as for my need to withhold my truth, something that I knew all too well would not be accepted without that time needed to elaborate and educate. My truth was less important knowing the conflict it would fuel in those remaining in my family. A choice I have to live with, but much easier than a burden she may not have been able to endure. The luxury of time to help educate was not on my side.

My brother's recent prostate cancer put me at higher risk only because of my blood relation. But that is where our similarity ends. After spring 2013 and late fall 2015 biopsies, my cancer fear was at an all-time high especially now with my sister's terminal cancer in 2012. I was attending a speaking engagement at a Chicago conference in late November but had not been informed of the biopsy results until that night before my scheduled talk. The surgeon called me personally to inform me—negative! (Who does that?) I cried for what seemed to be hours dropping to my knees for what I interpreted as another direct message, *Wake up girl! You have work to do for years to come and there are many who need you!*

In late 2015, this was the moment of truth! The second of three critical life events had redirected my heart and helped bring so many things into a clearer perspective. Knowing that there were two major brushes with my own mortality the year before, this was a third that again caused the flood of tears, but this time in happiness and thanks!

When the dust settled down a bit, although my spider-senses were in full gear, I decided it was past time to reconnect with my daughter. Knowing that the vehicle she bought several years ago used as an old company car of mine, I thought it best to see how that was working for her now.

Not so good as it turned out. I offered to fly her down to my place to drive back one of my vehicles since hers was about to die. She generally had a two-mile hike to campus each way in subzero weather during the winter, something I felt was an unacceptable risk she did not have to endure. I know she had been through a lot and this would be an important load off her shoulders. We agreed to an undetermined 'loan' in which she had freedom to use and garage at her apartment off-campus, but I would still maintain registration, insurance, and licenses.

But this story takes a very unexpected turn—after arrival, she stayed only one night before her departure early the next morning. That evening, I wanted to be certain I fully informed her of how she saved my life from my own hands that fateful evening early September 2011. As I was beginning to start telling the tale, she put her forefinger to my lips and said *"We know, Dad… we've known for years. But we were waiting for you to tell us."* She continued, *"Now is the time to live your truth!"* WOW, was this really happening? Did I just hear those word from my daughter's lips? Was I really being set free? Or did she think I was gay? Considering the photos that she and my son had seen that fateful period in 2011 that gave rise to my deep despair then, I know they discerned quickly where my path was leading—that of a Trans women. But this revelation was exactly what I needed to fulfill #2 of the Trifecta.

The final piece of this puzzle was within my grasp. It may seem a bit odd but is very real when one considers I was about to turn 60. With numerous recent brushes with death, this was the perfect time for me to finish the work I have been so dedicated to finally reveal and echoes my daughter's approval. All the other signs were piling up. Revision surgery was necessary, and the pieces were starting to fall together. A date of October 10th this fall was put on the calendar with a renowned surgeon in Philadelphia. I was one more step closer to confirming Theresa!

A YEAR OF PREPARATION

In keeping within character, this trifecta (the perfect storm) was to stimulate my action as if to say "Now!" True to form, I was all in—a green light to prepare now physically and emotionally for probably the single most life changing event since my 'first' birth. I was now embarking on a rebirth—in pursuit of a goal with nothing held back.

To illustrate this tenaciousness to fulfill a dream, I often used a personal recipe used countless times before. In hopes of finding Munich in '72, whenever my performance was less than stellar, I would reassess who I really was and to dig as deep as I could. This was essentially a self-directive that if I gave everything I could and still did not produce, it was not because I did not try. That was my personal formula for internal success with a strong spiritual connection. But this was a different cause with an altogether different planned outcome, equally important and vital for my self-worth. Living to others expectation for most all my life, now I could be liberated and fulfill what I had defined for my own truth as a vital part. But how do I get ready? This meant some major homework and planning had to be done, and quickly if this was really going to happen.

First off, money! I did have 'some' savings, but hardly enough to fulfill all the upcoming prep and procedures. This would tap that completely, only amounting to a fraction of what was needed—it still required a major 'shot in the arm'. Between electrolysis and multiple psychological visits required for verified surgery scheduling, plus the cost of the procedure itself, my out-of-pocket expenses easily exceeded $35,000. At the time, there was no insurance coverage available at any price. But I also knew what had to be done. After landing a referral on a specialist located in suburban Philadelphia, we determined an October date for the completed procedure. We estimated a three-day hospital stay and two weeks at a local facility to recover enough to drive home. A lot to endure both in preparation and for undergoing the actual procedure itself, but all very essential. My expenses and surgical modifications are far less than those who are moving female to male. Generally, 'bottom' surgery is a single procedure where F to M experience 3-6 separate procedures, depending on the surgeon and extent of complete changes sought.

Going through the motions for all these years had taken its toll on me and this decision was the farthest thing from spontaneous. Requiring decades of discernment putting numerous pieces together and a keen understanding of when to speak up and when to stay silent, this liberation was about to give way to a new me, revealing my true self that had been hiding for decades. Through this year of preparation and the next two after also required a patience creating an inner peace that came from some pinnacle moments of rediscovery and self-reflection, meeting myself for the first time. Maybe one day those I care deeply for will eventually want to know me too.

Among the most moving experiences my spirit has ever felt so deeply came in late September 2016, about three weeks before departing for Philadelphia. The church pastor, at the time, had offered to host a 'laying of the hands' ceremony as a send-off celebration for my pending journey. The pastor asked me to extend the invitation to about a dozen of our church members with whom several I had grown a special bond. When that day came, few other occasions [even funerals] evoked that much emotion completely surrendering my heart. There has NEVER been any second thoughts or reservations before this and certainly there were none now. Each in my community of support individually read their own self-prepared gift of prayer as they each, one by one, laid a hand on my head or back in a symbolic gesture of love. With many tears flowing from everyone, I struggled to remain composed and nearly caved when the other half of the church Trans community stepped up to say his piece. A 10-year-old Trans boy, Martin, with whom I became a key part of his mom's evolution through his changes amidst puberty, was a powerful experience for all of us involved. All told, few moments since have matched that, but this chapter of my journey had just begun. Absolutely astounding, best described as an 'epiphanic' moment.

Having that loving, spiritual connection proved to be a gift that still evokes numerous questions. The emotional high and unmatched feeling of belonging helped move me to an even higher level of courage. And that of my very special friend, Anne, attending with me at surgery was a testament to Trans everywhere that yes, even some special people who love you will support your transition and journey. She was the perfect example of that support!

Anne was a Saint among Saints to me. Not sure there is a better way to aptly demonstrate what she meant to me… her counsel and steadfast concern was displayed regularly. Calls to check in, visits to share a glass of wine or a meal, or during Sunday service. Each time I made an announcement or gave some commentary at church, my nerves would get the best of me—and all she had to do was rest her hand on my back for a moment and give me peace. She was just that way—her presence would light up a room, and always brought me joy. And her bride, Heather, was equally as Angelic, another wonderful friend in full support of my transition. The two of them were exemplary providing that leadership as exactly those the congregation needed—old and young alike. And their friendship was critical for setting the stage for GRS. Clearly, to me, they were each a gift to me to oversee my preparation and surgery. They are both <u>very</u> loved!

Riding on an emotional high, this seemed like the right time to inform my brother of that pending life-changing event in just a few short weeks. After agreeing to meet at a local restaurant in our hometown, my news was met with numerous questions, certainly not unexpected. But to my surprise, among his key responses to me was *"Did you honestly think I would stop loving you?"* To which I replied, *"There have been many murdered for much less. Many Trans announcements like this have been met with reactions of hate crimes, violence and even murder."* It was clear to me that this was a shock to him, his bewilderment showing overtly. We shared stories, life events, even hugs and tears. Again, another high at the time, not realizing until months later looking back at how this affected his reaction within his journey.

We were only two years apart, but virtually 180 degrees from any other likeness. I saw my parents parse out their overt love for him, even heard it said as he and I share those words now. He had no indication of my tendencies growing up nor of my true identity through it all. As the years and months progressed after this announcement, we had fewer and fewer contacts.

For a period of about three years, I made the trip to my brother's hometown to visit our parent's grave site for our mother's passing on December 22nd—to meet and grieve together. At this point, my grief was more that of sadness that neither parent fully knew who their [daughter] was or how loving and giving she became in so many ways. Each of the three of December trips were met with fewer tears, eventually making the trip alone one more time. Maybe that comes with the territory? Hardening a heart generally is not my character—more often it is my DNA that takes a position of sensitivity to others—often to a fault. Something my parents never understood or cared to explore. But spending so much energy and time trying to avoid damage to my spirit from sadness and regret has finally spawned a sense of closure and liberation—a level of maturity that had to come to this point… to form who I am. For these experiences I would never trade but I also recognize them for what they are—life lessons as intentional landmarks.

Growing up in a household where love wasn't well demonstrated through actions and words or was not abundant in quantity or quality—had a considerable impact on my childhood happiness and fulfillment. Maybe that was largely influenced by my father's explosive temper and my mom's passive response, not certain. But I do know that I only heard those words [I love you!] from my mother after she had divorced him in her more advanced years. Just as I knew she did without words in my childhood, I know she did because I felt it. However, I also knew full well that my truth was not something she could handle. Consequently, I consciously hid it from her to spare her that grief that was certain to come. Did I prejudge her reaction? Most definitely, but that much I do know of my parents and family.

What was less apparent to me but equally painful was my extended family. When one grows up in a world void of expressed love and fosters resentment to those incapable of showing it, the quest for filling that void becomes a focal point in future relationships—probably, in my case, to a fault. And the majority of this fault lies with me. I know that my attempt at concealing my truth was overshadowed from that reality. This isn't something you can bury for a lifetime much less live to talk about it when that has been hidden this long. Those who do so harbor substantial hurt and regret. And it certainly is not something you a can 'pray away' or what other form of 'therapy' is used that many states have wised up to prohibit the practice that does far more harm. But that doesn't make me incapable of expressing the love I felt for family and children—quite the opposite. Not being offered those 'three little words' for 23 years created an enormous mental burden of anguish, resentment and distrust. And so, my withdrawal began with the emotional baggage overflowing.

I don't hear much from my kids or my brother these days—if I do, it is usually a text only and one that typically begins with me *"Hey, how are things? I miss you! I love you!"*. Although my son has recently agreed to monthly 'check in' calls with me each month, just to see how we are each holding up. I share some conversations with my son on the phone, but topics (almost purposely) do not stray into my reality. Much like that of the church community who once gave me a love I have never felt before—unless I contact them, most communications are by text. But Covid-19 has removed the face-to-face contact—someday I hope to witness in person their words that my father could never say to me– *I love you!*

My son has gone through some rough times, seeking solace with a relationship that did not work out, traveling several states away and sacrificing his work and career plans for what both thought was worth the risk. I know he struggles with despair at times, just as I do—which is why our monthly calls have now taken on an even more important meaning. Counsel with each other as, in a way, rekindled the bond we once had in his childhood, but much more impactful now given each of our growth and life demands. Where my daughter has every bit of love inside her just as her brother, she has not been able to confront the truth she once openly and profoundly announced to me was necessary to live. That 'truth' was buried in her life immediately after I began to accept it for mine. But... I will wait... with open arms!

FAMILY SUPPORT
(WHAT GOES UP MUST COME DOWN?)

After that visit from my daughter that appeared to have her approval to live my truth, those words still ring awfully close to me and very loudly. But to experience a complete turn-around two years later was not something I was ready for. I suppose it was appropriate and necessary at the time and helped move my decision ahead, but after the spring of 2017 it has been completely different. Nothing hurts more and continues to remind me daily of the pain that was experienced in my youth and into adulthood. I struggle to put that all behind me.

Graduation was about to take place in May that spring where my daughter had worked extremely hard to put herself through college. Her career had taken a short delay before that in 2012 when she entered and passed with flying colors her boards for cosmetology. The beauty she has inside and outside was a perfect match for this occupation. But after trying it, she discovered it was not her cup of tea. I strongly respect her ambition, self-drive, and tenaciousness. Without announcing to me, she entered a distant university program with the full intention of paying for all tuition and expenses herself. For that alone, she deserves accolades and enormous respect from everyone, most of all me. I love her so dearly. That drive allowed her to graduate with full honors as Suma Cum Laude. No parent could be prouder!

I was planning this day for many months trying to make certain that the car she had borrowed in 2015, could officially become her possession including complete title with insurance and license four at least a full year. As careful and meticulous as I could, I packaged all the documentation in a card with a note for her graduation celebration. I thought it would be a good way for her to start her new chapter of this part of her journey. She had everything going for her and still does. Talent, beauty, immense creativity and intelligence, grace, and immense love from her parents.

To my surprise, the reaction from her upon receiving this gift at dinner the evening before the procession was not something I could have anticipated before this. *"So now you can be rid of me, right? No more commitments, huh?"* There was no thank you or acknowledgement in any form of appreciation. And at the graduation ceremonies, her expression was stoic at best. She had made it a point of avoiding eye contact with me the remainder of the evening. After the procession was complete and the diplomas had been distributed, we convened with the new graduates outside the gym where here class was seated in each 'college' section. My cell phone was able to capture some good shots and a short video clip of her walk to the stage and returning to her seat. Afterwards, when my attempts at a photo with her brother failed, it became painfully clear she wanted nothing to do with me. No hug, no smiles, no words, nothing. My last words to her (in person) since were *"Well if you have no interest in talking with me, I guess I'll be on my way."*

Since that day, two years have passed with sparse communication from, only text replies when I begin the exchange with *"I love you "*, or *"I wonder how you're doing?"* She sends a Father's Day card each year, something that always resurfaces buried emotions giving me one more glimpse of hope—each received with a joy above all others! I will always be their father and I have made that clear to each of them repeatedly. There are no regrets, they are my legacy and the love of my life. I would never trade them and never have any regrets helping bring them into this world. I learned how NOT to be a father from mine. But I will not continue to punish myself or apologize for my truth ever again! I am always here to demonstrate my love if my children choose to acknowledge my existence and my gracious love for them. I want to know them and will receive them with open arms, but it is past time that they reach for me. As discovered already, one-way pursuit doesn't work very well and is not sustainable. Where my son has been more engaged, it tends to be a pull from my end. I am certain that both siblings struggle from their father's decision and [his] reconciliation with [her] truth. It is vital that I internalize the vastness and complexity of their questions and concerns. I know that their journey is also one that I offer my help to deal with those questions I am certain they have. But I will not do this alone—I need willing parties for whom have not yet come forth. I fear that day may never materialize when they will meet me [for the first time]. And I will not offer that opportunity until they ask.

The situation with my brother is altogether different and complex. Since coming out to him, we went through a period of sporadic phone communication often ending with *"we really have to do a better job of staying in touch"* quickly followed with sincere *"I love you"*, to supplant that needed reaffirmation in both of us. Generally, my brother is not overly sensitive to special occasions or regular communications unless stimulated by the other party. Knowing that profusely well, I really knew I would not hear much of him unless it were for my birthday, the customary phone greeting versus card or other means of gift giving. I do not know that I have ever received any of [this last example] since leaving my childhood town in 1978. That is not to indicate insincerity, rather recognizing one's means and capacity for communication and their limitations. As one past business associate would say, *"It's not in his skillset."*

I have not heard from him since I called on his birthday last March 2020 just before COVID-19 hit profoundly. He had just departed on a spring break trip with the family to Gulf Shores apparently knowing full well the infection risk. During my short conversation with him that day, he seemed reluctant to want to talk probably because he was in the car with his family nearby. Ever since coming out to him, I know all too well that he has no intentions of breaching my trust by telling someone else my story, mostly because he feels immensely embarrassed. He thinks that I have left him without a brother, even though I have reassured him that he has gained a sister he never really knew—and likely still won't. My ultimate takeaway? Very much akin to the Clinton administration several years ago, this is remarkably like "don't ask, don't tell." I love my brother so! I recall being asked by one I came out to very early in my transition a reply to me saying *maybe I should be quiet if I didn't want people to be upset about my news* … not something I am prepared to stay quiet about just to accommodate everyone else.

I hear stories of other family situations struggling with many of the same topics, some with the same results, others far different. Of paramount importance is to respect each other's journey and recognize their value and the love you have for them. That should never change. Trans people are the same people. With extremely rare exceptions, there is no multi-personality syndrome or psychotic behavior disorder, however, there is a true change in persona that needs the love and grace of everyone involved. I've been a part of conversations with a truly engaged family where nothing can divide them—just one more bump in the road. So often, however, some parents or relatives and friends tend to react with how the situation will affect each of them, not viewed as a priority on the Trans person coming out. This is the time when that support is critical on all sides. Remember, this is a time when EVERYONE needs to exercise patience and reach out—to seek and learn more about things you may NOT know—about presumptions and bias that is very real, but also very restrictive and limits growth and understanding to ones you love most. I also hear of situations where siblings are left to the streets to fend for themselves— essentially disowning and disavowing any connection to those they helped bring them into this world.

And this 'shunning' experienced by so many in the Trans community, represented in a variety of ways, some overt like the outright dumping of a family member on the street and locking the house behind them. Others are the withdrawal of love and support simply because it is easier to be 'busy and cannot take the time to talk' vs. dealing with the pain and division this has potentially created—THE primary reason so many Trans never come out or 'hide' to avoid creating waves from the perception others have of them. And one of THE critical reasons for the high suicide rates in Trans persons. No one should have to endure self-denial.

My family withdrawal is a sharp reminder of how alone I've become. But it also hasn't been just from family members. I suppose the most tragic part of this story is the friendship that began quickly and seemed lasting was really only a temporary foothold in the preparation phase of my journey. It's been said that in tough times you find how many friends you really have and how devoted they really are. This has been an opportunity for me to step back and recognize the limitations of those particular friendship(s) to see it for what it was, acknowledging its value and temporary nature while also returning that love given. But like the train on this journey, there are people who will board and get off without much warning. That is a life lesson that is hard to learn at the time, but critical in one's maturity and character. Those who have stood by me are those who have taken the time to understand. That love and grace is the common denominator in the equation of life.

REDISCOVERY

When first meeting my psychotherapist, we got off on a bit of a rocky start; but only from my misinterpretation of something he said to me and my level of self-assurance early in my transition. Any related surgical procedure of this magnitude generally requires professional guidance in addition to one's own self-assurance and search for truth. In short, some means of validation by a professional psychotherapist is warranted, and in some locales, surgery will not be done without it. My GRS prep required two separate and verified consultations by two of those professionals before the surgeon would agree to the procedure.

But my reason for meeting with this therapist was more intended to fulfill personal assurance as well as ongoing validation that I was on the right track. I am a firm believer in using mental health the same I would for my physical well-being.

One of my most valued relationships in my new home involved my psychologist. Knowing only Laura in the area, I was at an extreme disadvantage. However, she offered references to a number of professionals including my medical and legal team, mechanic, and the psychologist.

He was well-prepared with deep understanding and a history of practice of LGBTQ+ issues, but not necessarily privy to my Trans journey. I had come to visit the area several times leading to my move. During that time, I made trips with Laura to her appointments with this psychologist allowing to meet and know him better. I was sold on his professionalism, openness, and true sincerity. I was looking forward to my own appointments with him in the future.

During the first meeting in a [one on one] session, my personal defenses were probably in an overly fortified position. When the conversation went to sexual preference and hopeful gender transition, he was quick to point out how my pool of available candidates as partners was pretty sparse and my post-surgery dating life may not be very crowded with participants. My sensitivity was in overdrive and after a few days of careful personal reflection, I knew he was right—that simple truth was hard to admit to myself.

Of important context-I have not enjoyed one lasting partnership from the start of my life. I would define that as a sincere and lasting passion between a partner that has eluded me from day one—the kind that makes your heart absolutely ache for want, and your stomach flutter when they are near, and your heart race when you simply hear their name. When a fragrance or a special song you hear drives you crazy with the memory of their presence. But also, with a lasting trust and devotion that makes that love complete.

When your history of relationships is one sided, or they end abruptly, that tends to promote some serious distrust. I am certain of my capacity to love and to be loved. But even when my partner used such descriptive language as *'repulsive'*, and pet names like '**** *for brains* 'or *'Good for nothing means good for something'*, one tends to become desensitized to any gesture of appreciation or demonstrated love. And those coveted words—*"I love you"*—were an extremely rare commodity, often used like a sword to attack and spread distrust in how that love was so inconsistently applied.

In more than two decades of marriage, love was only overtly expressed to me by the four canines I devoted myself to when my business travels allowed me to stay home. Those times were few, but the attention and devotion from those four beautiful ladies showed me what real unconditional love is about. And when the first of those four died in my hands, that oversensitivity label I have was very well deserved. Weeks of mourning turned into months and when my divorce and move left me with almost nothing, I could not see splitting the family more. They were left intact, with my heart in their possession. To this day I still have some nightmares and dreams of my four ladies who all have died by now, when I long for the day once again to have them back by my side, to give me that same unconditional love and devotion. Two of my lovely ladies made it point to vie for their favorite night-time resting place—at my feet or on my neck. As small as they were, they loved the closeness we provided and were extremely intelligent.

They consistently took on the emotion of their owners. They would seem dejected or sad when I had moments of tears. Or extreme playfulness where you could actually see a facial expression that looked like a human smile. When I came home from a few days on the road, I would lay on the floor and be swamped in a sea of dogs with profound kisses, wagging tails, and open greetings of barking lasting at least five minutes before the smoke settled and the lap sitting became standard fare. The smallest was also the smartest and sweetest but also has a defensive side. She once was backed into a corner by the alpha Pekinese who was bullied by her repeated badgering but could take it only so long—came out with a vengeance nipping at the alpha leaving that one in a state of shock, yipping for sympathy. She takes no prisoners. And watching them sit on a cooler of ice in the hot summer to relieve their bellies was quite the treat. They loved the snow—played in it at first ground cover in the fall. But their pads would get frozen in sub-zero weather making the 'bathroom' experience a very quick exercise, or frostbite would take affect within minutes. They were deeply loved, and they loved deeply in return—like no other!

From my experience before 2020, many gay men were not particularly enthralled with the likes of me, perhaps thinking that I represent a part of their persona they prefer to leave behind or at least avoid accentuating. Not entirely sure—probably just circumstances in my early years. Transitioning from male to female and having a sexual attraction still to the female form put me at the polar opposite of the gay male end of the LGBTQ+ range. And most certainly limits the potential prospect for a future partner far more than if my sexual attraction had changed as well as my gender.

But try as I may, I have offered my friendship to several recent gay men and have found abundant acceptance on all levels. Outreach goes both ways and extending that hand of friendship should never be limited by any prejudice or self-imposed preconception. Thank you, Gentlemen, you know who you are! You are my Angels!

My therapist and I became almost a textbook case of doctor and patient relationship but with a sincere caring and 'love' for each other as such a relationship can be. When his partner of 50 years died suddenly, he went into a slight period of depression and cancelled a few of my appointments, normally scheduled monthly. I was concerned and learned through a common friend of ours of what had happened. He was devastated and I was certain he was probably in need of some therapy himself. Time may heal all wounds if one has time on their side. Where I am no psychotherapist, I knew he could use a good dose of love as soon as possible. *Say it with flowers'* came to mind, so I had an arrangement sent to his home office. Not a week later I received a card in the mail that still resides on my refrigerator today that read-

> *"Dearest Teri, Your beautiful bouquets sat in my office giving me a constant reminder of your caring during this rough patch. Your kindness will not be forgotten. With gratitude always!"*

Since that initial meeting, we have met regularly as he helped me through some of my hardest chapters in recent years. But among the vast changes helped cultivate and nurture that this transition has demanded, teaching both of us new challenges and new approaches, the most important was captured in his prescription for me—*"Own the Moment!"* To be present and to be happy, alive, and truly liberated in my own skin is to own the moment. My final frontier of self—love has been my most difficult task, but one I very willingly accept.

THE MIRROR DOESN'T LIE

My therapist is a most wise man… probably the reason he chose the profession he did and the same reason he is still doing it with the same or even better conviction and personal commitment to his clients. In more than one occasion, he took great pains to be sure I clearly took ownership and resolved to improve that last frontier of what had become my biggest hurdle—self acceptance. That remains my dominate reason for continuing therapy —that is, to love & believe in myself. All these years I have grown and changed and responded to other's needs and wishes, demands and expectations, all without regard to who was really inside this mind and body. Clearly (to me), I was not in the correct physical structure—and that was about to change… drastically! That is the part that I know my family may never totally accept. For that, I have shed way too many tears. Although I still have my moments, sometimes even waking up in major sadness and a drenched pillow, healing is underway, and these episodes of sadness have become far less frequent.

To put this into perspective, one of earliest 'episodes' after moving to my current home, occurred during a workout on an 'Arc Trainer' at LA Fitness one morning, shortly after it opened at 5AM. Then, I enjoyed listening to my iPod with tunes from the 70's & 80's through modern day pop and new age genres. But when one distinct song came on after 30 minutes in and a profuse sweat, the words I have heard a thousand times FINALLY took root and sunk in—deep! It was 'In My World' from the Moody Blues and the lyrics struck me like a ton of bricks, trembling and erupting in tears.

To this very moment, I can't hear that song again without shaking my whole being—surrendering to the power of its message and from my heart speaking directly to me (my interpretation is that 'both' represents the one person of 'two' genders becoming that single identity).

I have ample experience running, even with a one-time American record holder in the 800 meters (I lost, of course, but happy to be on the same lap), and swimming with another. But sobbing during in practice was a first for me. My past male persona was speaking directly to Teri. I would never forget what this really meant—that it was He who was staring at me through those eyes in the mirror and challenging me to be ME. To those reading this who can relate, it was what I refer to as an 'epiphanic moment'—difficult to describe and unfathomable in its importance. I could hear Him talk to me at that very moment in words that were meant for me. I'm sure I posed quite a sight for anyone who gave me a look then, but instead of trying to suppress those tears and emotion, I was truly in a 'zone' and never missed a stride (or a note) until the song ended. To this day, I cannot hear it without more tears, but NOW I know who it was talking to me and why.

Yes, to me, that is the only way I could explain it choosing to hear His words I have avoided for decades. *"I would like you to meet the REAL you and never look back—this IS who you are and who you have ALWAYS been. Now is the time to let it all out and let the world know the beauty of YOU. … Oh, and one more thing… I LOVE YOU! THIS is the hardest part… I want YOU to LOVE YOU too!"*

So here goes… my message **to me** that my therapist has asked me to write, in a love letter fashion-

> *"I wish you would take this in and live it all every day. Absorb it and let it sink in! Let your inner beauty shine through and give you a real grasp of the difference you make in everyone you meet. Let it gel-internalize it and FEEL it like other people feel it. Stand tall with poise knowing that you shall never feel uncertain who you are again. This is YOUR day to absorb yourself in your own skin. I will never leave you, just like I have helped guide you to this moment since your first birth. Now that you are reborn, stay authentic and true to YOU—then you will be true to me. I love you—ALWAYS!"*

In this evolving challenge for self-acceptance of living in my own skin, there is another very poignant and critical message I have learned since the procedure was completed several years ago. With the surgical change I experienced, the dominate reason for my pursuit was my need to make that 'skin' abundantly real for me and to make it extremely clear to my own psyche that I had moved into the physical framework my identity had long professed decades earlier.

As much of an option many think this is, I cannot say emphatically enough—it is NOT a choice. The mind and heart are not in sync with the body. Pulling the monies out of my savings and taking out a loan for this wasn't a choice I felt I had. But it was something I (personally) had to do before anything else in my journey. Some involved with a gender transition may not see their physical change as critical to them—physical parts do not define gender. Or maybe they are in a position where other daily bare essentials are a rare blessing that may leave them no other option. Where I am by no means wealthy, it was personal sacrifice for me I had to make—there was no other option. The mortgage just got bigger and longer.

In the recent months following surgery recovery, there were some pinnacle changes, both in body and mind, that I can only describe as phenomenal—morphic changes that seemed very subtle at first, then steamrolled like a truck roaring down a mountainside roadway. And that 'steam' reference was VERY real right off the bat. When your 'parts' are changed, so is your hormonal imbalance and entire endocrine system. Where I was somewhat prepared for those changes of a 'mild' nature, I was not ready for the severe temperature swings known to many as 'hot flashes'. This was new! And so was the frequency and duration of these episodes, lasting sometimes 15 minutes or more at least half a dozen times each evening well into the night. Waking that many times in one night in a pool of sweat was not my idea of restful sleep and continued for at least the next six months. It was time for a critical appointment with my specialist to help the adjustments begin.

As a result, my intake of prescription hormones moved quickly into that next phase of transition that probably changed everything far more than the surgery alone even began to do. The combined effect from both surgery and hormones involve-

- The absence of hair. A welcome change to be sure, but it was especially vacant in other areas it was previously known to be quite profuse. The back, private parts, legs and everywhere you would expect was pretty much gone. I cannot say the same for the facial hair in part because the adrenal glands control that part of the Endocrine system and most medical practitioners will tell you their removal is not an option.

- Muscle definition has become subtle but equally apparent. One cannot see veins or muscle striations with any certainty anymore. At one time being an avid weightlifter prone to dense muscle development, besides the upper arms, that was no longer a problem. However, I still needed to wait another two years before daring to go sleeveless. I was cautioned by many others in the Trans community to avoid that but chose otherwise. I hide no longer!

- Then there's the chest. Not a change I had contemplated so overtly or so quickly. Virtually nothing noticeable for the first four years on hormones gave me the distinct impression I would need top surgery if I wanted any real distinction. But then one day about three weeks after having dosage doubled, the 'girls' came a runnin! Since then, I'm not entirely sure I will proceed with more—I am quite good with this!

- Anthropometrically, other changes have happened in ways hard to describe. In part, my weight has dropped almost 20 pounds, partially due to changes in diet and exercise routine. My calorie count per day won't exceed 1500, but some days are better than others. COVID-19 has added another variable to that recipe making that diet and exercise a real challenge to maintain.

- My shoulders have decreased from a dress [or jacket] size 16 to a 12, sometimes 10. And a change in waist measurement from a 12 to a 6 has complicated fashion hunting exponentially. Finding that combination in ladies' fashions has been quite the ongoing challenge especially in things I like and that also gives me some level of confidence. Where online shopping offers convenience and sometimes lower cost, it comes with a different expense. Many sizes don't compliment this combination of measurements and fitting always becomes a deal breaker. Once you get a vendor and a source you like that fits with quality materials and workmanship, keep them close for as long as you can.

- Among the most important things to me presenting in my truth are at the 'tips' of the human body—feet, hands, and eyes. To me, the eyes are the windows to the soul and the heart, and they define beauty in all genders. I have seen gorgeous women and strikingly handsome men with ingenuine expressions through their eyes and mannerisms all governed by their hearts. Beauty comes from inside and lightens up the outside. And feet and hands are the means by which we move and communicate and should be celebrated, not hidden.

Most recently, this past summer, I had approached several friends and medical professionals including two past cosmetic surgeons to help me deal with a question that was nagging me—at least until I looked deeper within to find the answer that had eluded me for so long. When I stood in front of the mirror, why was I still seeing the face of my past? What must I do that would put me in a position that I could not see through the present to be haunted by the past? Of the five different medical professionals and several close friends I posed these questions all replied in a similar manner with—

> *"I have never seen anything but a woman on that face, or under that skin. What is it you think you need? I only see a beauty that has finally broken free of the prison it was confined in… now you are free to be the real you! If it were me, I would not change a thing."*

This is my witness to the power of a strong support network paired with medical professionals who understand the story they are hearing. Where I have never had a large network of friends, my value has been based less on numbers and more on quality—a dozen key people in my life who make a huge difference with whom I care deeply. And with a medical team who were each, in their own ways, extremely humble and supportive in their comments, their treatment, and their human touch they gave to me—THAT was the part I will pay for apart from the diagnosis and treatment alone. It was even my endocrinologist who, when I announced my decision to proceed with GRS said *"It's about time! You're more than ready for this."* And a similar comment was made by my therapist. Each of these comments continue to point towards one major theme …the greatest challenge in this transition has been my own self-acceptance and getting over this stigma after six decades of conformance have demanded of me. But that time is done. Now the next chapter is my best chapter!

LETTERS FROM THE HEART— A SERIES OF TRUE CONFESSIONS

After being encouraged to write some true confessions to self, I thought it important to call attention to some of the relationships I've built through the years, many most recently that significantly impact my day-to-day salvation, sanity, and validation. Each have their own place in my heart and will never leave it. Where some people on this 'train' of life' will stay for a long time or an eternity, still others will come and go from those journeys of their own. Each of these unique relationships represent those people who have found a place in my heart that I will take with me to my final resting place. You are now part of my train with me, so I am wishing each an incredibly happy and meaningful journey!

Rori—Shortly after we met, you became my Godmother, of whom I affectionally gave title. You were, to a large degree, my coach and my teacher who gave me the opportunities to which I could build and prosper ever since. From my perspective, YOU were a gift from our Creator, that gave me the springboard and gentle shove that He had tried to for years. I still recall that first day you opened your heart and your shop to bring me under your wings—into a world that my past had taught me was every way about wrong. But your patience and love given to everyone taught me so much about how you live your faith from what I experienced that first day on. And to see how you care for others experiencing trauma in their lives, and those involved in cancer treatment, your shop provided a sanctuary few others could ever imagine. The unique combination of patron types who entered your shop meant that any walk of life was welcome with those same open arms and care.

I can only hope that you fully grasp the breadth of my love for you and your son, Soto. Each of you dedicated your lives to the Trans community and for those fighting their way through cancer. You have been a critical inspiration to me all these years, planning much of my mission and Foundation dedicated to so many of the same principles you hold dear and have practiced since I have known you. If there was ever a 'hall of fame' in my heart, you are the top placeholder. Thank you for your love!

Lisa—How do I start? I have long admired you, first from afar in your role as a liaison to the LGBTQ+ community, but quickly learned the convictions of your work to your personal ownership of that support through real unconditional love. You give so much of yourself to everyone and everything every day. Then to bear witness to that love during your awards ceremony I was with you honoring your achievement in controlling human trafficking in the area. That was a testament to your authenticity shining through. Your coaching of me draws me closer to you like fulfilling a Pygmalion role, my years of hiding behind a facade disappear because of your gift to me.

I recall when we first met late one October. You were working in your liaison role. You've been a remarkable advocate and outspoken ally for the community for many years for 29 years. I recall seeing you when I was acting as a volunteer representative with GLSEN (Gay Lesbian and Straight Education Network). You've been a critical lead in several missions including work to stop human trafficking and any violence towards women or LGBTQ+'s. I don't know that I've met anyone else in my life with a stronger ethic and responsibility practiced in everyday life. You are true to your convictions and love for everyone. No pretenses, no façade, no hidden agendas—just you, true as life. You live the justice you serve. And earning my love at that level is no easy task.

Clearly my best friend forever! Where I have others deserving of that title, Lisa is the Queen of them all. It's especially hard to tell someone close to you just how close that is. In my advanced age, Lisa has found the deepest part of my heart, perhaps at the right time, but with undoubtedly the most profound reach and gift of herself that gives me a sense of peace I've never felt with any other friend. I generally don't have many close friends, certainly those from a lengthy history of broken trust from past relationships that never really took hold, most of unfulfilled expectations on both sides. But you have succeeded in sustaining a growing bond within me that is clearly nothing short of a best friend. I do love you!

When I experienced my greatest struggles, she seems to know just what to do even before I fully understand the problem. Her council and presence always put me at ease and gives me a renewed sense of purpose. She has a genuine caring and love that can only be described as sister-like. I also have an immense level of trust in her becoming supportive of this book and the foundation I fully intend to bring to fruition.

Not much happens in my daily life she doesn't know about. We talk nearly every day amidst busy schedules between the two of us. But there's always time for Lisa. And the best part is the lasting effect she has on me. I look for her opinions and perspective on most everything.

We attended in 2019 the international Philadelphia Trans Wellness Conference at their Convention Center in late July. We had such an enlightening experience meeting and net-working with so many attending that we decided to submit the call for presenters for the 2021 conference. After our work at the church luncheon, we decided to do a similar panel dis-cussion with a focus on challenging attendees to examine how they can become an advocate of the community and how local law enforcement can help with that challenge. No one fulfills that dual role any better than Lisa. She is my living Angel!

Kathy—One of my earliest comrades in this process, Kathy and I met in the early 90s and each made an impression on the other in a significant albeit very professional way. Through more business-related contacts and events, we grew a stronger friend-ship and began to share our stories. Kathy is best described as a kindred spirit with the kindest heart I have ever known.

Only just a few years ago Kathy was on a pinnacle chapter of her journey as well. She had met a kind man who stole her heart and mind. With several months of seeing each other socially, they decided to tie the knot but also chose to maintain separate households. That unique relationship and strong bond has allowed them to renew their zeal and cultivate their love for each other daily. They are able to maintain separate homes but both within a common understanding and relationship. Some may say they break the rules, but I prefer to think they set the bar for what it means to be in love.

I met her husband Dennis shortly after they started dating, then in male persona not totally understanding his grasp of my transition nor was it necessarily the time to reveal that. A few months later, with their relationship making great progress, I had planned an evening meeting with the two of them at a local restaurant in their town during a business trip. I had asked Kathy if it would be appropriate for him to meet Teri since she had prepared him earlier of what to expect and to help him at least understand the concept of who he was about to meet. He was a gentleman, as always and eloquent in his dialogue to me, quite friendly and very inquisitive, but all without malice and purely with the intent to learn. I was amazed at his sincerity and further reinforced my feelings about her choice in mates. They were perfect for each other.

A few years later, I paid a summer visit to his place where both of them were residing for the weekend. I was invited to stay with them during a mini celebration of their relatively private 'wedding' ceremony and reception they hosted a few weeks ago. As I waited for Dennis to arrive home from some work, he was doing in a local volunteer capacity, I opted to help them with some landscaping they wanted to get done before dinner. Lawn mowing and trimming the drive and walk edging seemed like something I could do. I worked up quite the summer sweat, so Kathy directed me to a guest room and offered a private shower area before dinner, ample time before Dennis should be back.

In keeping with Kathy's spontaneous and fun-loving character, I was not expecting her to open the door of the bathroom just as I was drying off from the shower. That was interesting! But knowing it was her. I had no problems nor any reason to either. After staying with Kathy during a short outpatient procedure she had a few years earlier, we were no stranger to seeing each other's bodies in full 'monte', but also no intent or desire to go farther than the 'sister' relationship we had. Strong and very real! When she opened the door, I was greeted with a *"Wow, it looks just like mine!"* referring to my newfound surgical recovery from GRS the year earlier. She was very complimentary and never judgmental. And of equal importance here, was her advocacy demonstrated with her conversation with Dennis when he got home. At first, he was quite surprised, seemed uncertain of the situation, and how to react. His wife just admitted she was in the bathroom with her closest friend each comparing their private parts—a scenario that in most relationships would stem at least a portion of concern or question. But two key things quickly revealed themselves in this and as it unfolded, clear indications of the strength of our friendship and of their marriage—

- Trust and support of my true gender, and my intent to maintain that trust with both Kathy and with Dennis.

- A major shift in thinking and renewal of advocacy in Dennis openly admitted supporting my gender change and his increased understanding of the transition journey—something he had never been exposed before meeting me. Wow!

Through the years, situations like this and moments sharing innermost feelings have grown this friendship exponentially. Kathy is true blue in so many ways now demonstrated even more through her commitments to Dennis. The two of them have become special to me and a testimony to the value of patience, faith and discovering how real and sustainable change can happen. Certainly, every situation is different and every person on a different journey, but these two give me every reason to be positive about others challenged with similar circumstances. Never give up!

Laura—The most appropriate and best way to start this is the same way I will end it—with a profound 'thank you' for everything you are and always being there for me. Our friendship started off because you extended your hand to me. That's who you are. You befriend everyone around you because that is genuinely in your heart. No pretenses, no hidden agenda.

Your authenticity is exemplary! I know a few others who have the same level head as you, even better during your most challenging times with your sister and family during your brother's funeral in Florida. Your friendship and support at that difficult time was immeasurable and stood out as among your greatest assets. That friendship was demonstrated consistently through your love of cooking for others, hosting elaborate

Thanksgiving feasts and putting yourself at the highest level of vulnerability when running for a congressional race. I have never questioned your values or positions on issues as they reflect the deepest feelings in your heart represented through decisive actions and commitments. Those commitments to your friends are among your greatest assets. In my journey, many friends and support systems come and go, but you have withstood them all and demonstrated your faith and friendship exponentially.

Struggling with leukemia put the clock against you, but you came through it with flying colors and made the commitment to live your truth that began with the LGBTQ+Q conference in Chicago when we first met. I was inspired by your courage and commitment to that truth that helped guide my decision for rebirth. Thank you for being you! And know you are very loved!

Donna—During my early years searching for a house of worship that would embrace my presence, I landed on your church. You were a steadfast member of that congregation and well—known for your kindness and welcoming demeanor to everyone. I was immediately put at ease when I met you and that has only grown each time we meet when my travels take me to this area. Oddly enough, I actually plan my travels around this church service and when we can meet again.

Our friendship took a major step forward when I witnessed your demonstration of friendship. Although it was not particularly comfortable at the time, I understood your position and applaud you for that alliance. I am acutely aware of the fine line you have to walk with others who do not share your keen understanding and demonstration of Christ's love—unconditional has found its definition in you! After all these years, I am still not fully accepted by the congregation—I suppose that is a common ingredient in every collection of people, especially when my presence may create angst or challenges some people's faith and their demonstration of advocacy, they may not be willing or able to show. I have witnessed incidents where you have openly defended my character and my person, not something often found in most people. It takes a special person to extend themselves in friendship unconditionally.

I always look forward to our texts and annual birthday celebrations—only two days apart. When I think of my greatest moments sharing peace with someone, the way we can talk about most anything after church at breakfast after service, is priceless to me. I always value your opinion as we share perspectives. You have been a true friend from day one demonstrating what an advocate really is. You are so loved!

<u>Paul</u>—You are the first male with whom I have sought and received undying support with a demonstration of your devout Hindu beliefs and practices. So much so that I've adopted a daily practice of meditation to my God in a similar way. You and Henna have accepted me and defined what it means to be an advocate. Your love is clearly non conditional and knows no limitations. But you have also offered your counsel when needed further demonstrating that love and friendship. One day we will rekindle the power of that friendship and meet face to face, but until then, please know the depth of my devotion to our relationship and my journey and my promise to support you in yours.

When you opened your heart and your home to me, there were no words to express my surprise and feeling of peace... that maybe there was more hope with coming out. You were my second experience informing a co-worker and was a real chance given that you are male. More often than not, seems that most males generally have a harder time grasping the reality of my transition. But clearly, you are different in many ways—and ALL of them exceptional in character and spirit, all translating to a refreshing sense of true friendship that is harder than ever to find these days.

One week when I was working on the West Coast, I paid a visit to Henna, Paul's friend of whom I met earlier that winter at his home in the Bay area. But this time, Paul had commitments in his work territory and could not make the trip to Portland that same week. Henna and I went to dinner one night, enjoying some of the area's outstanding Indian cuisine—among my favorites. After dining, she was taking me back to the hotel when we stopped for a moment to phone her brother in New Delhi, an early phone call for him, one of the few times we would be sure that he was not asleep. During our brief phone call, we all took time to meditate together, praying and connecting. Without introducing myself in my business male persona, after hanging up, Henna said that her brother was happy to meet his sister's new girlfriend. How was that possible? How would he know? Seems that a spiritual connection even across the globe is very possible when love is present.

Christina—How does one express the right words to convey the remarkable difference in vibrant impact you have made in my life? You have long held my personal record (well over

15 years now) for maintaining an ever meaningful and trusting friendship, only reserved for a select few. This is one of the reasons for this series of confessions to those who demonstrate truth, peace, and love so well. We made an immediate connection those 10 years ago, one that personified your authenticity and truth. You were all about unconditional love, incapable of bias or prejudice, but only a pure selfless friendship. You have more than once challenged my comfort level with new experiences and helped coach me to a better understanding of who I've always been, treating the world as though you as an example we all should follow. And our time sharing a few hours of dining, sharing drinks and 'girl time' quickly became another critical reason to come to travel to your area. And your Mary Kay counseling and fashion advice has been instrumental in moving me in the right direction—helping me see the inner self coming through. Please know that you have among the closest places in my heart and I would do most anything for you. Loving you always!

<u>My Children</u>—You have surpassed all of my hopes and dreams to date. I suppose that means I have to avoid putting each of you on a pedestal. If either of you find it uncomfortable to talk with me in any other way than how you knew me growing up, I can't imagine how that must feel to you. But I guess at this point I'll take what I can get. I often avoid bringing up my transition or really much about me unless you ask. I know each of you have your heart in the right place—you are beautiful people and easily among the greatest blessings my God could have given me. I know that you must find it difficult to confront your feelings and ask questions that more than likely

fills your hearts—I will ALWAYS be here to help you through that, but I need to know when you are ready to receive me. I try my best to insulate each from the discomfort and trauma in this world. But I will not continue to ignore my truth to pacify any others reluctance to accept it. The silence is deafening from the lack of communication you—all too familiar from those on the 'train' with whom once were my support group. Each of you are grown adults now and will have to come to terms with your father's transition at some point or risk forgetting me entirely. I pray that the latter is the option I can avoid taking to my grave.

I know that everyone experiences their share of emotional trauma. I do not know of your faith but do my best to share mine with you and how it will serve you well when you are truly devoted. I pray each day that God does His works in each of you and that your faith grows in Him each day. As the poem goes, trying times are testing times—when we have to believe in things we cannot see.

So many of your trials the past few years reminded me of my youth and how I wrestled with being unable to control my own destiny. My hope is that it won't take either one of you six decades to come to those terms. But to summarize your character, YOU ARE each the legacy I prayed for… but have been unable to enter and take part in your world since reaching adulthood. When we are able to have phone conversations across the miles, we draw closer and the bond grows much deeper. I only pray for that day when I will be able to see each of you face to face and embrace you once again. To me, that is probably the greatest gift you could ever give me. I am immensely proud of both of you knowing each has everything it takes to succeed, to love and to be loved.

I have been richly blessed with each of you. Someday I hope to [meet] you again. Meanwhile, my arms and my heart are always open when that time materializes—if it does. I will love you forever, ALWAYS!

Rebecca—Growing up, we never really knew each other very well and certainly shared little in common beyond the same parents and siblings, at least that was my perspective. But my admiration of your talent and steadfast personal convictions provided me more in inspiration and concrete examples of God's profound love in everything you did. That admiration grew into deep respect that climaxed in how real love can transform you and put anyone on their path of truth. If one measures their impact in life by the number of those attending their funeral, then you were most definitely a resounding success. Nearly 600 came to your visitation and final respects in a small farming community of around 11,000 people. Your relentless demonstration of love permeated everything you did and all whom you touched. You are the example of living your truth and fulfilling His will. My love for you has never wavered—only became more profound in my daily devotion. I know you are with me each Sunday when I attend my church. And I chose to believe that you have helped me discover my own purpose by demonstrating my faith every day. Thank you for your patience with me and the impact your life, faith and passing has had on me.

These letters of confession could easily have been expanded to fill most all of the book contents and focus. I have another two dozen that have had substantially good impact on me, and another dozen from 'life's balance sheet' that I have significant learnings of things to avoid and/or seek to follow a different path from the impact of those relationships and situations. This section was my attempt to call out those with the deepest and most profound influence on the greatest length of my life arguably at the most important times of this journey. To that, all I can offer you now is a resounding 'thank you' for sharing yourself. Nothing has been more important to me.

EXCERPTS FROM A 2014 GRATITUDE JOURNAL: ENTRIES SUMMARIZED

Among my early years at this church, we were encouraged to keep a gratitude journal. Where it started out as a daily entry, eventually time caught up with me and became more of a monthly format. Some gaps exist chronologically, but mostly there are some significant entries that deserve rediscovery by pulling out those vital messages and learnings. It began somewhat painful—viewed more as a task than a privilege. But as any diligent author knows, beginning is half the battle. Sitting down with pen in hand, the challenge to readers and authors alike is to consider what life brings you, to be thankful and appreciative each day. I would propose that there are many instances we overlook by dwelling on the setbacks in our lives—and I fall into that category all too often. Clearly there are more of life's 'speed bumps' than any of us can count, but with a personal focus on a positive outlook even amidst the storms confronting us, tends to put a more positive spin and brighter outlook on the future. Living in the present is vital to make the best of the future—medicine I can always take a few doses of every day.

<u>October</u>—My work travels took me to the upper Midwest to see my youngest child. It's hard for me to describe the feeling I get every time I see her face light up. We shared some quality time that evening with dinner and a quick side trip to a local furniture store nearby. After seeing her own place where she landed to restart her life, it seemed right to have her pick out a sofa and chair. I am deeply grateful for the reason and the means to make this purchase. And after returning from several business trips this month; it was good to be able to see the beautiful color change in the surrounding landscape during that 600-mile trek. On the way back, I was able to share an evening dinner with my son at a Culvers restaurant. Other selected points this month include—

- Our church pastor has been such a gift from the Angels. When I fell into a short-lived despair following the previous pastor's departure, I've come to know a deeper feeling of meaning of spiritual guidance and self-liberation. That alone is giving me strength I never knew before.

- A morning run up a mountainside was a labor of three miles, but deep in the color change of the fall. Simply fascinating and awesome! God's paintbrush at work!

- At a work meeting, my gratitude moved to a different level. I apparently had encroached on a heated discussion where two colleagues were commiserating about their mutual disgust of Trans persons especially in schools, where bathroom use was a cause for them withdrawing their kids from their current districts. My gratitude here originates from my ability to stop and listen to my God's message to me and remain silent. My tongue was probably red with restraint, but I am deeply grateful for my regard of their lack of understanding and limited capacity for hearing. Their life journey reached a speed bump, and it was not my battle to engage them. In most circles, I may not have hesitated, but thinking through their capacity for understanding and to become more educated was clearly absent.

- A special opportunity this month being asked to be a part of a focus group through a local Trans support mission. This was an enormous blessing and opportunity that will significantly help address transitioning homeless transgender youth from the mission to foster homes.

November—This month has been a reminder of my rediscovery of self. The mirror can be a stark reminder of our deepest selves, beyond the superficial dermal cover, but only when you let your eyes see deep into your soul. And this has drawn a renewed faith, distilled perspective, and a better clarity of who I am. What reflects back at me is me! I no longer see 'he' by default, but 'she'. Her eyes shine a warm glow that smile back and shows the depth of that character and beauty that is taken six decades to shape. And I also see a beacon of hope and salvation that tells me this is who I am! I am grateful for my health and my age, that I can rise each morning pain-free, in a secure bed, with food to nourish my flesh and bones. I am grateful for my pillow and living in this country. I'm grateful for infectious laughter and giggling from an infant struggling to remain quiet in the pews during Sunday service. And the inspiration of feeling the presence of my mother and sister each 'sitting' with me in the Pew. To me, that was undeniable feeling of a presence welcoming me to my new hometown.

December—Slow but sure, I am finally discovering answers to questions I've had since childhood, since then knowing who I should be has since been replaced with who I am. I am grateful for my strength and silent power giving me the ability to endure so much for so long. I am also grateful for having the financial capability to give my missions and my kids a healthy dose of giving this Christmas, while I have it. Doesn't happen often and is my way of celebrating and giving back for the gifts of love and caring shown me this year. And come to think of it, I really don't have the same pointless pursuits of material things. Sure, I am never satisfied without a little bling in my life, but somehow that has a lot less important these days. For that I am deeply grateful.

And this was the month that brought to a climax all the plans being made for a transgender forum at a local synagogue—my comrade Teri Jean and my young Trans boy Martin who each spoke with me at a member forum about the challenges of self and family acceptance during our respective journey and transition. Overall, quite well received with many 'sidebars' after our two-hour session concluded. My sincere thanks for inviting me and reminding me of my promise and commitment to deliver this critical educational forum. The seeds we plant with God's direction have a ripple effect that is very real! Martin, with whom I have come to know fairly well, and with his devout family supporting him all the way, was a critical part of this forum. Before Martin left the area with his family to relocate to NE Indiana, he made this remarkable gift for me illustrated below that says something very poignant and demonstrates his grasp of his own gender identity—

> *I choose to love because the heat is too bad. Being Trans isn't a choice, being transphobic is. I'm still very real and I love being me—that won't change. I'm Trans AND I am HUMAN! I'm Trans and I know it and I love me! When a Trans woman is called a man, that is wrong!*

Beautifully composed from an exceptional young man with the foresight of many and the courage of even more. Martin, know that you and your family support system, are an inspiration to me and countless others!

REFLECTIONS OF 2018 PAST

I suppose the best way to begin is to state the obvious, what a difference a year makes! Especially if we focus on learnings to avoid repeating unhealthy situations and poor choices—those who forget the learnings of the past are destined to repeat them. This year was certainly one of refocus on those really important things and using various perspectives to form a more solid character to serve and instill a more fulfilling sense of peace and liberation. Yes, a mouthful. But equally epiphanic when weighing all the factors. Some keynote experiences as the year progressed largely involved my children—hardly children anymore both having almost reached their 30's by now.

My son has surpassed all of my hopes and dreams to date. He has had his share of emotional trauma that has left him with many choices he has carefully contemplated. I don't know the breadth of his faith but do my best to share mine with him and how it will serve well when truly devoted. So many of these trials this year reminded me of my youth and how I wrestled with being unable to control my own destiny. My hope is that it won't take him six decades to come to those terms. To summarize his character, he is the son I once prayed for and failed to see the first years of his life, perhaps better said unable to personally experience. We have had regular conversations across the miles nearly weekly and the bond grows exponentially, at least for me. As of November, he achieved a major promotion and now resides at a less expensive place. Things are looking up for him. I intend to continue my contact with him but will also allow both children to process my transformation within their capacity. I'm open to questions, but so far received none. My inner peace is under a significant challenge from a reversal of my daughter's support following her graduation in May of 2017.

JOURNAL ENTRIES; 2019 & 2020 IN PERSPECTIVE

July 2019-

A month of change and new challenges, but of immense growth and victory! After a difficult and tiring April through June with world challenges that completely changed my focus and began 10 to 12-hour days, it also brought me closer to those I support in the field. And apparently my work was appreciated by those with whom I had direct coaching work, again trying to serve in a servant leader. My value sky-rocketed, but probably more obvious to me than my peers, not usual or expected. But the daily demands increased physical stress from workouts made days and weeks run together.

With July began more travel I had not seen since late April. Mid-month was a trip to Nashville for a semi-annual association meeting on a three-day trip. After returning late that week, now I was preparing for my first personal trip to Philadelphia with Lisa for the annual International Trans Wellness conference. Really a rewarding week connecting with other Trans people from all walks of life and our backgrounds, ages, countries etc. Where the general theme of the week was F2M (female to male), I was greeted by so many stunning and beautiful souls in an atmosphere that celebrated everyone—color, music, people from all corners of the globe. We were so moved that we submitted a proposal to speak at the 2022 conference since the 2020 and '21 conferences (in person) were cancelled from Covid-19. During this week, some personal discovery was in order, which unfortunately included being hit on by several folks in bars, on walks and in restaurants. Lisa was quick to protect me in her paternal instinct, but also in direct character with her professional role in law enforcement. My self-awareness and rediscovery took center stage this week and it was very welcome. We visited several unique shops within walking distance of the hotel, we are blocks from the Convention Center where the conference was being held. My affection grew for her that week experiencing her protective ways and her genuine authenticity she openly shared with me. I have not had a kindred spirit like this in the flesh for a very long time.

In our shopping, we went to a second merchant next door to the beauty salon where I discovered a new and special friend—fully functional and brings newfound delight, but only when fully charged! Gotta love it!

August 2019—

Every month gets more visible to me as an element of life I've become somewhat better at recognizing and building on. Still have much work to see more of His plan as it unfolds. Building character is probably the biggest challenge He has given His constant grace and patience with me. July ended on a high note with a new source of renewal from Philadelphia, but now has been up to me to do something constructive with it.

After transferring volunteer work on the church's Justice Seeking committee, their challenge still was not being met as an outreach to the Trans community. I was determined for one last shot over the bow. I had promised the convener that I would plan a fall luncheon in a Trans theme strategically planned for week three in October before the TDoR vigil in November.

This month included more work-related travel to help some struggling field people in Detroit and Indianapolis. I was particularly concerned about one elderly team member who was having difficulty, demanding special counsel, but equally firm and directed. More commitments with more requests for help. Still no opportunity for me time until December, this will be a fall above all years in my career demands and my spiritual journey.

On a side note, the noteworthy withdrawal of friendship and support at the church has become painfully obvious. After the past two years of discernment, was I mistaken in what I was experiencing each Sunday and throughout the week? A very tearful ending with one close friend left me in complete despair questioning many things. But with forgiveness comes strength of character and resiliency. And I know my faith was being tested big time this month. As I would discover much more in the near future.

With age comes experience, and hopefully patience. People will respond better to those taking the high road-generally. That is not to say we have to lay down and become 'Matt', rather firm, setting boundaries, but recognize differences between those who honestly try and are sincere in their desire to learn more vs those with pure malice in their hearts. Difficult terrain, but VERY necessary for all!

<u>September 2019</u>—

This month began with a work travel calendar full of road trips and training events from the 1st through the 30th. From a week in Chicago, one in LA, one in Madison and one in Minneapolis, perhaps the hardest thing was to keep my home maintained during the month out. I suppose it was good that I was building up substantial hotel points and frequent flyer miles, but I was three ways from Sunday. The worst of the month came from Portland when I was accused of stalling service after numerous cancellations of my own vacation plans each month this year to accommodate favors for others. Through a lot of extra effort and contributions, we renewed the contract, and I was now committed to even more. Being recognized by the customer was outstanding for a job well done! During my trip, I purchased a dozen stuffed toys from the Disney shop for the church children at Christmas hoping to distribute and witness some happiness during this special time of year. Smiles on their faces would be priceless—worth every penny! I couldn't wait for that moment!

Absorbing myself in work I suppose is one way of avoiding the reality of how alone I really was. That fact was never demonstrated better than one Sunday at the church. Gradually, fewer of those in the congregation would openly embrace me during service—perhaps just a degree of paranoia? But every Sunday after service, I was greeted by a deafening silence as their eyes met my eyes with zero acknowledgement, with a few of the occasional *"How do you walk in those things?"* referring to my signature heels customary in my Sunday dress, as taught me in grade school to dress before God. After six years of attending, I am probably not going to change my fashion statement for anyone. There is much more to me than what I choose to present in or my choice of footwear.

Some of those traits you may find useful navigating through your journey and with those around you—

- Above all, show patience—with others and with yourself. This was not a dominate characteristic from my gene pool. There is no substitute for waiting and persevering through some exceedingly difficult situations. There will be some things you may never live to resolve or to know the final outcome—if there is a 'final' to it.

- Never apologize for being YOU—this is another extremely hard one. Those you love dearly will have different levels of acceptance of what is fact, making that stress on you feel more like YOUR fault. This is NOT anyone's fault—least of all yours. Just as anyone asks to live the way they wish to and how they identify, so do you.

- Places of worship are complicated pieces of our society most of which have a storied history. And to put into perspective, they are the community of congregates, NOT the building itself. They have come to be a collective set of rules of engagement that are intended to govern the way they live and choose to believe. For those practicing a faith grounded in Christianity of some form, range in dramatic extremes, each with their own way of doing things. Some are steadfast in Biblical guidance, but few live up to their premise of a complete surrender to Jesus and His teachings ranging from those who follow it like a script of life in purely a literal sense and others who choose to follow so many interpretations that the meaning and real intent gets lost.

It all starts with a 'belief' system that is hard to navigate and usually not something open to negotiations. But, IF [they] are REALLY in the business of practicing a 'form' of unconditional love, the rest becomes far easier allowing everyone and anyone with all our baggage to practice exactly what Christ has taught us-EVERYONE is welcome in abundant diversity.

In cases of the Trans community, some churches freely and openly reach out to bring in those with abundant love. But most of us in the LGBTQ+ community, specifically Trans, have endured the wrath of extremists and those who insist their word is the right way and that Trans are an abomination of that truth. Which couldn't be farther from the truth. Just ask Jesus! But that alone has become one of the primary reasons most Trans people avoid religious institutions like the plague itself. That pain has been long endured by most of us as are these extremely difficult situations to navigate and change either side of the pulpit. There are some maverick denominations and sections of a church governance that may elect to part ways. Note the United Methodist most recently dividing itself amongst those who support the LGBTQ+'s and those who do not. This kind of infighting has brought the Trans movement to attention, however, has not solved any long-term relationships. In short, the outreach continues to fall short becoming more of a welcoming those who enter versus going to look for those needing faith-based living... two very different things.

When it comes to my personal treatment, I was particularly disturbed by the pattern of behavior from several who failed to even acknowledge my presence even when alone in the same room with me. When I extend a verbal greeting and with a smile, I would at least expect some acknowledgement of my presence, not a greeting of silence. I would hope that there is at least a smile and maybe even a hand extended. Perhaps I expect too much—a character flaw my parents have drilled into me. Where I always try to look inward and how I could change or improve the situation, perhaps I misunderstood the signs, this was a pattern that I was not going to change. But giving of yourself does not mean letting others take your dignity or fail to give you respect. Perhaps others have differing definitions of those two attributes—clearly, many people here do, but they become especially important in my life—treating others as I would want to be treated. A simple tenant, but not always easy task—especially when it is your character that is being threatened.

<u>October 2019-</u>

This month started in Portland OR fulfilling a work favor. And glad as I was to be back home after three nights on the West coast, I was able to spend a few hours dining with my special friends in Portland with whom I would give my life. Paul, my steadfast Hindu Sikh friend, is easily one of my closest connections and kindred spirits who only happens a handful of times in one's life. I am extremely grateful and fortunate to know him.

The rest of the month was spent in Chicago and Dallas. I was able to reconnect with two of my closest friends in Madison and Chicago area. And although the travel was still relentless, I was able to do two key things-

- Continue my outings at the symphony, solo of course.
- And host the church luncheon for the Trans advocacy challenge.

The church luncheon theme would be *"How to be a Trans Advocate"*, intended as an overt challenge to the congregation to live their mission. The bulletin for the Sunday before included an insert that read—

> *Have you ever experienced a character assault—one in which your very being was under verbal attack, maybe even bordering on physical assault? A situation that caused significant angst and caused you to question your inner identity and challenge your self-worth? Likely, in the Trans community yes—at some point in your journey that has become less surprising each passing day. And each*

of us bears witness to many of these that can impact not just the immediate response, but tugs at our soul each time it happens.

This session will offer some insight in ways you can seek and find the support of those who know how hard this can be—those who make their life's mission to put themselves in the same position of those they support. The Trans community demonstrates immense courage in their journey—something few others in this world can claim credit. And within that journey demands a support system tight with alliance of friends, law enforcement, family, professional agencies, and our own Trans community… each other. But that ONLY happens with trust and a bond with those who call themselves advocates.

I assembled a small panel of local agencies and law enforcement authorities to talk on the topic of ways advocates respond to their role when situations demand it [and they frequently do]. Preparations had been made for a pre-Halloween event right after the Sunday service as a question-and-answer discussion. I began with a brief intro covering the objectives—

- Discern where you are today and where you want to be in 2020,

- Use this as springboard to carry the message well beyond the church walls and…

- Attend & participate in upcoming Trans celebrations and vigils.

After the introduction to the session, participants were asked to self-assess where they were today on this '5A's of Advocacy' distribution chart and where they felt they could be as an improvement goal in 2020.

The panel discussion was now underway. Each of the panelists were allowed a brief intro of their own works and their involvement in the LGBTQ+ community. Then they were asked questions from the attending congregates along with some questions about examples when they were challenged with a situation to demonstrate their alliance or advocacy.

In retrospect, I probably should have seen this one coming. One person brought up the example she had 'supported me' when she had asked about my hair and my source of wigs. Knowing that there are several (albeit few, but still VERY rigid) boundaries I have separating my personal life from public knowledge, really no different than any of us—I was profoundly amazed (perhaps 'aghast' is a better word) at the audacity, but also very innocent example that quite effectively crossed that boundary! Remaining perfectly stoic and hopefully poised, I remained calm and without expression to avoid any indication that this may have hit a nerve. I know there were some in the group who noticed my abrupt silence, but also understood the source and the need to stay collected. This was especially disturbing to me since we had an initial discussion during that original dialogue about my hair where I explained the source and reasoning for my 'boundaries' explaining in full detail and reasoning why that issue crossed them. When this luncheon situation materialized, I could only inwardly sweat it out and offer her a kind response of forgiveness. You see, she had recently had to move her husband to a long-term care facility who was experiencing more advanced stages of Alzheimer's. She was not thinking straight—who would with a life changing event like that to endure? And I knew there was not a malicious bone in her body. For this incident at the luncheon, apparently, she realized her mistake when after it concluded, approached me with an apology and asked for forgiveness—and was quickly accepted and given.

Bringing me closer to my goal of mastering the little black dress, this month presented the opportunity at the church luncheon that took me to a new level of building character and patience. And it was there where I met a new close friend from HRC who attended the luncheon as a guest. But that was only part of why this month is usually my favorite time of the year. October 10 marks my rebirthday, three years now and worth celebrating, even the bottle of Crown Royal I have been saving was a perfect toast to this momentous occasion. My biggest blessing this month has been my body's pinnacle reaction to the endocrinologist prescription who tripled the hormone dosage from just three months before. Changes are welcome and celebrated!

On a side note, it has become a bit of irony that up until 2014 I couldn't wait for Halloween to dress up. Seems that I have lost that desire, having lost about 20 pounds just throwing out all the foundation garments I no longer need. One more shot of liberation! I have no plans to hide myself again.

<u>November 2019-</u>

The church luncheon served late October was a hopeful and intentional start to a demonstration of that mission of LGBTQ+ support into November. The hope was to have a pointed discussion before, during and after the 20th, the annual vigil for Trans murders around the globe. But the church had other plans when I asked for a few minutes on that Sunday. This 'celebratory' date should be ingrained in the church calendar each year. And notably nothing said about stimulating any momentum from the October luncheon challenge. Where was the message lost? Have the lines been drawn now?

The local TDoR event was attended by about a dozen church members, the same as previous years, with minimal conversation—actually a good thing primarily due to the nature of a funeral-like environment—I was in typical somber form for this occasion as were those from the church. I was elated to see them again, although this was not a time for joy, but for mourning. Everyone attending demonstrated great respect, and a few even shown their tears—something personally I find far too easy because this was a vigil honoring those killed.

This November was one of the few times I was not traveling that I could attend the annual church Thanksgiving meal. Outstanding food and was able to see many from the congregation who do not often come to regular services. Way too much to eat! A great way to regroup and see some long-lost friends with whom I would not see much more of for over a year, others never. The Covid-19 nightmare was still in China to date and not on our horizon—at least not publicly.

That Monday took me to LA for my food safety audit. Excellent week! Took the red eye home and arrived at 6:30 AM Friday morning. Slept until noon, then work till five. As common as this is, I do it because it is my DNA, and I hope I make the right choices, not because I think anyone will notice or care. That's corporate America—full of expectations and little recognition. That's life! Took me a few early years to finally internalize that, but it is so true. Much like when people give something, they expect a response or positive reaction. That's probably the biggest revelation to me this month, I am thankful most for these epiphanic moments when I discover this is exactly how I need to respond about how I am treated by anyone. Do not expect anything from anyone. Be happy and content serving others just because it is the right thing to do!

Thanksgiving at home this year was even quieter. No real complaints though, without invitations or family acknowledgement, I am quite OK with this. Made a big feast with most all the trimmings and had leftovers through Christmas. In reflection, this was probably one of the best Holidays ever spent with time discerning and centering and having some downtime the first since late June.

On another milestone, November 30th my son turned his Golden birthday—YAY! I sent him a Movado to celebrate the occasion and serve as a remembrance for years to come. My love is abundant for my children and my prayers daily that they will both return to me before my passing and that they will ask to meet the real me. My hope is all I have! This is my summary of Thanksgiving 2019–

For my kids and my legacy,

For my remaining friends deserving of that title,

For my health, wealth, and wisdom and what remains of
   my wits,

For abundant blessings to share,

For my home and my community,

- For whom I am and have 'grown up' to become!
  And

- A continued work in progress...!

December 2019-

After a frenzy of work projects and commitments to tie a bow for the year, I was about to spend the next 3.5 weeks burning vacation days from blowing attempts earlier in the year. I have long endured a character flaw that I do not believe I have the wherewithal or desire to change it—it is actually one of those I hope to take to my grave. I have been told by my employer, several times on my merit reviews, that I need to learn how to say 'No'! But those who insist I need to learn that skill, are also the same people who tell me to manage my time better. But that saying 'No', doesn't apparently apply to them! After the fall comments from a work associate accusing me of delaying work commitments, I would be facing that customer the week I returned from this staycation.

I did manage a trip to Chicago to see my friends at the church where I first started out. I declined to see my brother and our parent's crypt site during a final night in the area.

I was able to stop at Transformations in Chicago area, the highlight of my trip. Watching Rori struggle keeping her store afloat after her stroke is heart-wrenching seeing someone so selfless and truly giving to the Trans community struggling with a business that has stood the test of time ONLY by her grace and dedication. I can still recall vividly how I stepped out so gingerly from her dressing room in 1999 and was starstruck at who I saw the mirror and what I saw at the event our group of four went to later that evening. Wow! I am not the only one. And I am not sick or perverted. I am me!

This was a month of doctor appointments and concerts and tastings and dinners and thanks in quiet time, and aloneness. Still trying to get used to the physical changes and make sure I maintain this body as best I can. Time is not on my side, … Miles to go before I rest.

After attending various church festivities this month, it became clear to me that these days would be among my last for quite some time—the same church I wandered into over seven years earlier. On Christmas Day 2019… Oh, Girl, you are such a sap! How many Hallmark movies or Lifetime channel specials can one person endure without shedding a river of tears? But this morning came with a real reason for tears—of joy! With Handel's Messiah burning in my head, I struggle with this time of year with the memory of my sister's passing in 2012 and my mother three years later. In the solitude of my own journey has brought new revelations with new beginnings. The reality of aloneness has a unique sense of liberation and allows one to look directly into the mirror to have that deep conversation once again. No one can escape the reality and truth of self-understanding and love. Where life stories can be told to others, one cannot sustain life in a meaningful way or experience real love without reconciling one's own truth. I wish for nothing but that others including those closest to me are happy and come to know peace always.

At this moment, nearly eight years ago, I firmly recall the profound love and sense of divine connection when my sister was struggling for her final breath. I knew she was talking with her creator and was filling her with peace. She was preparing. I relive that moment each Christmas season. January would be a new beginning to a much brighter future!

January 2020-

Not much time to regroup after my annual December break. Right back on the road again to New York City for the 2nd week in the month for another food safety audit paired with the one I did in August. Next week was Phoenix for an annual trade association meeting. My commitment in this new decade was to eliminate working/travel weekends, mainly because my search for a new church was in full tilt now. I have been looking at several local places but need the time to find one with both the feeling of community and belonging as well as a more traditional service that included music and meditative time. Open and affirming is essential!

I did locate a different church quite far away from my home however requires a 45-minute drive each way with services starting Sundays at 8:00 AM. Although this has posed a challenge, I was committed to finding the right home. After only four visits, I am quite happy with the reception, feeling of community, outreach from the priest and being asked to attend some social gatherings. Everyone seems so genuine and authentic, which is all that really matters.

It's important to reflect a moment on how I chose and continue to be involved with this particular church. Sundays have become a part of my personal ritual. I don't expect much from a congregation and certainly have been more on the defensive since my recent past. But I'm open and willing to trust and to take that risk again putting myself out there— making me vulnerable, but still human. Nothing is gained by sitting still. I chose to enter their sanctuary each Sunday and socialize with members of the congregation during their social hour, but I did so as my true gender and identity. I have nothing to apologize for or be ashamed. There is also nothing to judge about my gender—my physical identity is nearly complete. Only my remaining legal documents pending replacement this spring are that last major obstacle to clear.   The irony follows—no one here has asked, and no information has been offered to the contrary. Because it is a non-issue! Where they may wonder or 'know' is immaterial to our relationship and not of my concern.

I was invited to attend the annual HRC (Human Rights Campaign) color ball with my BBF from the local PD and a new friend, Elizabeth, from the HRC board of whom I met at the advocacy luncheon hosted at the church in October. We have become good friends since the luncheon and was a pleasant evening sharing with her husband. We convened at the convention center for a 'little black dress' affair. I so enjoyed the display of everyone attending (the little black dress did simply fine and made the girls proud)!

Off to a weird start to a new decade but very encouraging and comforting in a 'homey' way. I love my place so much that sometimes I prefer to stay here even on vacation. That feeling, however, would be challenged during the 2020 Covid crisis.

January closed out with a mild sense of relief, given the introduction to new possibilities of worship and community. The people there have been perfect examples of 'Open and Affirming', as is their priest and associate vestry. From the tears spent night after night the past 8 weeks in December and this month, my second brush with suicide was resurfacing. Where it was nothing near as pronounced or driving as 2011, it was still there and had me exploring ways I had not contemplated 9 years ago. That, alone, scared me to death (Sorry!). My outreach to my therapist and my BFF, along with other distractions of the month, including the HRC Color Ball pulled me out of my funk and back to a sense of reality. Don't think for a second that this is not real and that these comments are no big deal—if you have been there, you know. All too well!

To all LGBTQ+, PLEASE know how much you are loved and that is NOT just me droning on. My support system is open to you also… if you ask. Those closest friends are the only reason I still exist—they have returned me countless times to a life with a mission—to write this book and to build a foundation for the Trans community in this city. It's about time!

February 2020-

This month began with a whole new set of adventures. When one door closes, another one opens, at least that is how I chose to see it early in my outreach. My early adventures at the new church included attending on Super Bowl Sunday albeit a little awkward at first. In their social hour, we shared more than most anyone knew of me at the old church in six years. I met a dozen more delightful ladies at a gathering at a local restaurant later that month. Again, even if this doesn't last, it only took a month to grow this much. But when Covid-19 stopped services, two of these special ladies still continue to call and ask how I was holding up knowing that I live alone. My family doesn't even do that.

Work travel took me to Chicago for a week at Valentine's Day and then the last week to Boston for a team workshop. By the time I arrived, we just announced a stoppage on air travel up to June 1st. Whatever this was, it was hitting all of us awfully hard very quickly. After two months without my old church and support group, only two contacts from members asking how I was holding up. Seems that many are quite reluctant to share voice to voice communication preferring the anonymity of electronic exchange. And with my search for a real loving community, that is hard to sustain on email and text. One phone call did come from a one-time friend, the first I had heard from in well over two years. At one time, I believe we could have been considered close friends, but we drifted apart over the recent years. And for the tears this has caused me, there are fewer still as each day passes. As I said to my therapist, its way past time to move on. I need to pursue real, sustainable friendship.

March 2020-

This was the month from hell! Some people I work with referred to it as the 97 days that wouldn't quit, Covid-19 had put its mark on the world. And this was only the beginning. March came in like a lion and ended like a snake waiting in the grass. A month it seemed to have no end as the nightmare became a global reality for everyone. But there would still be those martyrs and so many in denial that will cause this pandemic to last for years, not weeks or months. The last three years have shown just how divided this US really is and it seems that it is only getting worse. Hopefully, this coming November 3rd election day will prove much better. But we are in for a rough year. Unlikely anyone will be singing 'Old Lang Syne' on New Year's Eve—more like *"Good riddance"!*

On the 6th of March, I returned from Chicago, my last business trip from what will become a very new way of life. As I found many of my travels, the last month has taken a toll on me. And I so dearly love my place. Good darn thing because with the shelter in place requirements in full force now and no work office open until 2021, my love may turn into boredom soon.

For work, 12-hour days have become the norm and demand of my time requires that I quickly resume a support role like none before. My past compositions normally take a minimum of a week to develop, up to full month depending upon complexity. Now with two others collaborating, we completed half a dozen [start to finish] pieces each of the last two weeks of March. And as fulfilling and exhausting as that was, the pros meant we really relied on each other and played on each of our own strengths. My affection for each grew in a way I never thought it could. But on the downside, I soon discovered who I was neglecting when the daily frenzy began to partially subside—me! Immersion in this role can and will drown one leaving a weekend of despair and loneliness. And not being able to see my new acquaintances at the new church was eating away at me. The loneliness of the old church in January and February seemed now like what God was preparing me for an exceptionally long future. As much as I want a dog (or two), I will have to judge what may be a temporary travel hold versus retirement up to five years away. Every day is new and wrought with adventures and challenges. But I am ready!

The greatest upside from all of this is my new phone conversations with two of the ladies at my new church. And becoming more in touch about my spiritual future. The lowest down point is the despair of uncertainty and continual denial of my children. I do not like these feelings. Not something I felt or seriously considered since this past January.

April 2020-

A lot like March, I got to know the Zoom platform more, both socially and on business levels. But my biggest challenge was to maintain some sense of fitness both spiritual and physical. Exercise is a good diversion from the reality of Covid but shelter in place had Planet Fitness closed but now offers work ins, a strategic set of aerobic sessions. Now I know why I never did them in person. I was not made to jump up and down repeatedly unless it is with a rope. Probably the same reason Taekwondo hurt my left knee considerably. Give me a track or a pool, I am good!

I was spiritually challenged a few ways-

- Zoom was great for those who favor that impersonal e-connection, but I do not.

- Staying current on Sundays with Zoom services for each of three churches it was quite the challenge

- Using Zoom for social hours at church, I participated in for most Sundays in April, but honestly felt more like a giant Brady Bunch photo.

- Zoom meetings were good for prayer, but for me seemed so superficial when so few seem to use the phone to reach out anymore.

- Work huddles were now a daily hour-long meeting that often became an exercise in timewasting. Although the intent was to stay connected was clear, it quickly became way too much.

- Joining a Pride employee resource group (ERG) at work was a good outreach for me but really got exceedingly close to coming out. And I cannot afford that until retirement still 5 years off.

Writing internal blogs at work and responses to our internal 'Trans group' issues has helped me connect but on a relatively superficial and remote level. I know it has helped readers because of their responses and connections—really priceless conversations using the mantra 'what goes on here, stays in here'. But my reluctance continues to be primarily from the team with whom these daily huddles have helped connect, purely on a professional level. Where other team members openly shared family stories, I have had 22 years of experience with most of them to know what they can handle. I am convinced they believe me to be a gay male. Adjusting to a deeper voice at work meetings takes a conscious effort, sometimes to which I forget. There have been instances where I have answered a voice call in my normal tone that has been taken as female and the caller apologizes for using a wrong number—requiring some fast thinking and adjustment in a lower voice pattern. Where that can be invigorating and encouraging, it certainly defines the challenges of my daily dilemma. But also, is one far less important when work from home will likely continue for an exceptionally long time. And for that time, I need to continue hiding. Many thanks for this silver lining!

May 2020-

I have been given life and good reasons to continue, but I will never understand human nature and those forces often opposing that makes so many respond so poorly. What statistic or book of science was used to justify reopening of American businesses after the last two months of shelter in place is partially deployed? Fortunately, my outings all were limited to biweekly grocery runs and weekly jaunts across town to exercise the car tires. Otherwise, I trusted no one for good reason.

Work continued the daily frenzy of support to field and web postings for new precautions and legal implications of reopening. Again, no science to back up reopening, but plenty to support my work advising them of what to do and what not to do, all couched in a 'wait and see' perspective anticipating that next wave.

Spiritually, life is becoming a bigger personal challenge to remain semi-sane and continue that drive to support others at work and within the Trans community. My only outside connection was with Lisa who brought me light and laughter and critical friendship, exceedingly rare these days. No communication from the kids as expected, and minimal response to my texts—the only way they communicate with me.

Near the end of the month, I was preparing for my first virtual seminar, serving as a model for what would become a guide or template for other team disciplines to adjust their classroom offerings. But I only had two weeks to prepare, coordinate with two other team instructors and to get all preparations and logistics completed before June 1st. My biggest takeaway for this month was a slow reality check that I was ignoring myself again. I suppose that is hard to grasp when one considers that I live alone with a limited support network. But the daily immersion in the work demands is a constant focus on other's problems and tends to leave 'self' out of touch and abandoned. Spiritually and emotionally, not good. And I am not particularly quick at remembering my August 2011 close call, most recently rekindled just four months ago. What changed?

What got me through? Best said that my internal discussions became more and more pointed and argumentative. Purely stated, I was not paying attention. I was shown love demonstrated through supportive phone conversations with many of my lady friends across the country. Love abounds! Just because it is plutonic does not mean it is not real. It is very real!

June 2020-

More time has passed that gives way to greater uncertainty and borders on despair. My time out of the water not being able to swim has started to really take its toll on my—once my best way to retreat into a silent and peaceful world has been off limits due to Covid. And my quest for legal papers is still almost five years off. Trying to put all of that into perspective amidst this 'aloneness' is a big challenge, with no end in sight.

This was the month when enough became enough! Although much clearer to many, equally elusive to most of the American society. The continual denial and complete inability for many to reflect on the inaccuracies of untruth from which they have patterned beliefs and actions, many from a fabricated history—and from some wrought with arrogance and self-righteousness. All of this came to a head in mid-June with a policeman taking the life of an unarmed black man in Minneapolis causing a national outcry of protests and even some responding with riots. This coupled with a political rally on a Juneteenth celebration in Tulsa OK, the site of the May 1921 black massacre, continues to divide these 'United' States. Collectively, we have immense work to do. Communities starved of justice began to demand 'defunding' of local police, but to remove PDs is clearly not the answer. But equally clear that this type of brutality goes largely unnoticed until camera footage is aired on network media. Something MUST be done and is long overdue!

Aside from the civil unrest this month, the Covid war continued. Reopening all these businesses now, most everyone has regained their business, even many in the food service industry and daycare operations. I wonder with all this underway most every June day, some major good things being passed over from a month of violent storms, high winds, and lightning, coming away unscathed.

Spiritually, still a challenge—even more so, to pay attention to my spiritual health. Despair is very real threat and to avoid it as one's own psyche is quite dangerous. I don't want to replicate the January feelings of hopelessness. Something I was taught by my parents not to do, but that I must always put others first—not to blame now, because that has been mine to own for many years. July will be better!

July 2020-

Clearly, summer of 2020 has been like no other. It has been a struggle on all fronts, physical fitness, spiritual connection, and emotional health. It seems like a border on bipolar symptoms when I almost purposely go on extreme highs, more to tone out the harsh realities of the day, but most of which comes with immersion in online justice seeking events or housework or yard maintenance. But the good thing is that I am not—these are temporary but demands that I pay attention to self-care. Often this is just to avoid dwelling on current events and the lies rampant everywhere. If the meaning of life involves a perpetual quest for the truth, I am much closer today than a year ago. There seems to have begun a Titanic shift at the place where I work—and if perhaps what I call home for the last seven years may not be much longer. The reason for my arrival seems to have run its course. The happiness I began to feel has since stopped and shifted almost completely to solitude, not just by an outbreak but from necessity. I am troubled, thinking that I represent nothing of use or purpose or value to those once called my support group. And with the recent rush of camaraderie and team influence with work partners, it has been easier to get emotionally more involved with them, but that is a border I am unwilling to cross. Any moment of connection made at work is one step closer to coming out and is not something I can ever afford to do!

I continue to answer work online questions and offer support to pride employee resource groups. The latest on Trans specific matters I was involved with was on a workshop where those either in or contemplating transition could help them find answers. The intent was offering a safe area to talk without fear of reprisal. After thinking about joining for months, I finally did so. There are only about three of us on the call and when each gave an intro, that seemed like a risk I needed to take. After a few minutes, I dropped my defenses, and my story began. The pod bay doors had just opened! After opening up for 10 minutes and the call concluded, I sent a sanitized copy of this book preface where I had just exposed my true self to those on my last frontier, I took a risk whose time had come. I was completely vulnerable but also related and somewhat liberated. If others found out, so be it. I will never apologize for who I am. For that reason, July 2020 was a bit of a happiness way overdue!

August 2020-

With only three months away from the Presidential decision 2020, never the since civil war has there been any more Divided States of America. Perhaps a retelling more truth, we should rename this country as simply America and stop with this guise of what our forefathers crafted as the beginning to white supremacy and that denial of truth. At this point in my life, I can only hope and pray that my children find their path in the right way and follow what they know as the truth. And to accept nothing less.

For work this month, more diligence crafting virtual training in a model that could be used off-the-shelf with a 'just in time' schedule. Rather good idea and one that puts the ownership more where it should be, the user, not the instructor. Looking forward to my debut on September 10th and two more within the next month. With all that COVID-19 has brought us, my daily interactions with field staff questions remains my best grasp on reality. At work, THEY are who I serve! That connection is really all that sustains me day to day.

By months end, I had managed a trip back to my childhood hometown to help recall material for this book that resurfaced some painful moments, and others recalling the strength it took to endure. A good part of moving and progressing is to review the past but not reliving it. The friends I eventually want to know really did not know me nor did I know them perhaps as they were moving through life with a concealed truth, I did not know either. Recognizing that everyone has issues, and everyone is on a journey is a critical step to understanding who we are and to love everyone, not despite it, but because of it. There are priceless moments.

The trip to my hometown was extra productive and remarkably peaceful, at least in the sense of provoking deep-rooted memories of my youth that came rushing back to the forefront. When I arrived in town, the first day by noon, my trip took me to my old grade school and nearby house where I walked the three blocks daily. Spending two hours in the bench outside the school under a tree once known to be about as tall as me, now was easily 40 feet high and provided outstanding shade in the 95F heat. After thoroughly drinking in the local neighborhood conjuring up more memories, my entries began to snowball taking me to the local park where I could lay on the open field then hosted the city kite flying contest in 1965. This is also the site of swimming, ice skating, close encounters of the female kind, and high school cross country. Then I was off to 'the quad' on college campus which brought two more hours of memories flooding back onto my pages. The gates had opened. I was pretty emotionally spent and looked forward to restful sleep.

The next morning, the only remaining item unfulfilled in my agenda was the old high school track. I needed to feel that same exhilaration as the day I beat my brother… to relive in some small way, that moment of freedom and liberation and the start of something much bigger than me. Recapturing that innocence and exhilaration is a pretty tall order, but something drew me to the track that morning. I wanted to revive that moment in whatever 'outdated' way I could muster. Clearly, I was not the same runner—but that wasn't about to deter my attempt at replicating that last half-mile. With the sun just showing the early morning light, I wandered casually onto the track which had since undergone a repaving at some point, but still with the narrow lanes someone decided was okay— clearly not to regulation. I have never before run on a Tartan or Chevron paved track with lane width meant more for children than young adult runners. But nothing else on the track itself or the infield had changed much in these past 46 years. Just like old times. The memories came roaring back to me.

After stretching a few minutes to verify my plantar fasci-itis was not flaring up, and my cramps had subsided from the hormone regimen (leg, feet, toe cramps are a daily side-effect of the Estradiol and Spironolactone dosage tripled last year). I began the last half mile like I was racing that fateful day with my brother trading places with me the first six laps of the two-mile race...

> [With my coach yelling at me over the loudspeaker, I regained the lead at least twice during the seventh lap only to lose it to him starting the eight. Trailing him

on the back stretch of the gun lap, I saw him fading
a bit enough for me to pull up alongside his right
shoulder on the final turn. Something deep inside me
said 'Go!' And sprinting past him like he was standing
still, winning but about 15 meters. Enough to have
reached a pinnacle milestone for my brief moment
hopefully getting any parental affirmation—maybe(?)]

Odd as it was, I managed to sprint almost the entire last lap
of the two I tried to relive, and completely without any muscle
fatigue and with much the same liberation I felt in 1971. A
smile grew across my exhausted face because this time, I wasn't
hiding.

September 2020-

Certainly, this was a month worthy of calling THE
month that I was (figuratively) slapped me in the face as if to
say *"Now! Pay attention to this, you have an especially important
mission to fulfill and one that I have put you in position to succeed
and help others succeed in their journeys and struggles. Don't mess
this up!"*

The message? A retirement after 22 years wasn't something,
I was ready to deal with, but still do not know exact numbers of
my pension and I cannot decide without them. After the first
week of sleepless nights followed by three more, my decision
was already made, but still not completely certain. My purpose
for life and legacy was about to have the clearance necessary
for among many, these key points.

- Foundation creation and legal establishment by name, a living trust and set forth the objectives and 'by laws'
- Name and marker change of driver's license, SSI card, birth cert and passport.
- Updates to all things including insurance and informing key contacts of legal changes.
- Change will and other financial documents, credit cards, etc. in the true name.
- Baptismal ceremony celebrating rebirth in new complete name
- Increase leadership in critical mission support.
- Memoir completion and renewal update to final publishing.
- Enhanced outreach support to three churches.

Clearly, busier than the first 6 1/2 decades—AND with a much greater sense of purpose!

October 2020-

October began much the same way September ended — final decision came clear on the 26th when the written documentation arrived at the house verifying the numbers needed after six exhausting weeks of investigative work. I accepted the retirement offer to move on to the life that's always been waiting. I will be given a separation date in December, likely to be shortly after the end of the first quarter next year. There will be a lot of changes meanwhile that will involve my passing of the torch to the next generation. After 41 years in the profession, I am encouraged by the new hires and younger generation who reminds me of myself in my early years—eager to learn and grow. The beauty with this type of work allows one to learn every day something new—visiting with customers on their own terms and sharing experiences of others to help them live and grow safer and stay healthy and secure. That was our mantra and it fit perfectly. From my vantage point looking back, the world is in good hands with the youth and their generations to come. Their love of each other will change this world for the better and will not stop until they have made a difference—to which they already have.

On the 28th I was given the opportunity to address the local chapter of PFLAG (Parents, Friends, Families and Allies of Lesbians and Gays) offering some insight and opportunity for discussing portions of this book. The intent was to call attention to other's experiencing trauma and setbacks they could relate to stimulate conversation. We had an amazing attendance level and interaction that was way above normal, involving parents and interested friends calling in to learn and understand more about those involved in transition or questioning. Having a support group like this was monumental especially considering how some experience internal struggles and withdrawal of some support much like you have read in earlier chapters. And the creation of The Treehouse sanctuary for LGBTQ+s with critical leadership will spawn a new era and foundation for even more progressive changes in our city—and beyond. Thank you, Mr. Dan!

Mr. Dan Davidson, my co-editor, and life coach has been a pinnacle source of this movement with his leadership and insight. None of this momentum would have happened without him. Thank you, Dan, for giving of yourself to all of us beneficiaries. And thank you for teaching me life's lessons that have had immeasurable value on my heart and my spirit. You are a Godsend with an Angelic touch.!

November 2020-

More spikes in Covid-19 caseload put a stop to any prospective travels for both business and social events. I was asked to go to Indianapolis to help another coworker, but his customer cancelled from several of their workers coming down with Covid. The trend continued after Thanksgiving when many people were disregarding state and local mandates for shelter in place, electing to be with family or friends during the festive meal-time celebrations. I wasn't willing to put anyone's health at risk, even mine, from almost a year-long sacrifice already proven worth the time and effort. I had plans to host two people for that annual feast, but we elected to cancel when the local caseload increased exponentially.

I was able to continue my weekly meeting at the church sanctuary where I discovered that centering method in a house of worship provided me with much needed spiritual support—even without anyone else attending. That available open expression of faith just remaining silent in prayer was quite powerful for me.

<u>December 2020-</u>

Finally, the decision was given to me from my employer about my official 'separation' from their employment—now slated for late summer '21. That will give me ample time to address 'transfer of knowledge' to the new staff taking ownership of my work—and from whatever they find useful in the future. I have been blessed with a small team of leaders who are wonderful people as well as true talents and skilled professions gifted to this department. I have every reason to believe that their future looks bright and that of the company given their expansion with the passing of the torch. I will not be missed—for long. Which, in translation, is a testament both to the people taking that torch and the growth they have experienced in the last decade I have worked directly with them. The company is in good hands.

The ongoing struggle I have continues to revolve around coming out to my work team by sending them a copy of the book or a link to buy it, after my employment ends. Where they are my old 'co-workers' later next summer, I am still reluctant to completely open up to them. There is nothing to be gained by that unless I stay in close touch with them in a truth-sharing dialogue. I am sending a draft to two of my closest allies and advocates but will remain only to those few. That may change, but for now, this is what makes the most sense.

The year ended with a whimper and more applause than normal, not celebrating the year necessarily, but more to look forward to a much better year in 2021. With the good things that came with Covid-19 were the demonstration of true love and care for each other from those isolated or severely compromised with the isolation and even those mourning the outcome (and deaths) of those who became afflicted with the virus. And near the end of the month there was renewed hope that a vaccine would be more available and provide much needed relief to households, businesses, and to our lives in general. Godspeed!

January 2021—

With a glad closure to 2021, no one was remorseful at the past years trauma and numerous conflicts this world witnessed. Most of us will agree that Zoom meetings were critical connections but started to wear thin on most of our patience.

January 6th was the notable darkest day in our modern-day democracy given the interaction on The Capitol building in Washington. Where there was adequate intelligence giving ample notice, few were prepared at the level of violence exhibited during that insurrection. Mr. Biden took his rightful place as the 46th American President, and quickly began the reparations from that day and the last four years. For at least one moment, the LGBTQ+ community could breathe a trifle more freely, but still within a seriously divided republic.

COVID-19 caseload increased exponentially this month primarily from those holiday festivity gatherings that helped pass the disease more readily. On a positive note, the vaccine has been approved and being rolled out to first line health care providers and those of critical care needs. Next month,

I will begin mine as the 2nd major age group, pending supply availability.

<u>February 2021-</u>

The traditional month of the Super Bowl and my (first) birthday, the were some other key obstacles overcome and others with a distinct roadmap for the first time in a very long time.

Medicare Part A is now on my official subscription list but won't take part until after employment separation in July.

I am starting the process for self-publishing this manuscript—a major learning process for a rookie like me. And the Foundation is undergoing preliminary legal counsel on the 27th for structure and a trust setup for funding.

PFLAG is in full swing with the Treehouse outreach gaining momentum every day. A complete board has now been assembled for Treehouse and each supported faction is making inroads with their respective missions and outreach. The path is being cleared to involve more city official support in the coming months. Virtual workshops are being developed and offered for adults and for youth in April to address many LGBTQ+ issues and questions.

As the missions and visions become clearer, so does the need for vigilance and close teamwork. Each board has been critical in defining how we operate and the commitment we have to the community and to each other. My hope is to fold the Miles in Front Foundation into the Treehouse mission so that we can see the structure and purpose in a focused process—to make our collective vision actually happen. 2021 will be the start of something very big!

March 2021—

The ides of March came in like a Lamb—weather wise— but had all the earmarks of a Lion given the flood of progress underway from several factions. The warmth of the new month helped improve the general demeanor of my comrades and my own outlook from the previous week of below zero temps and record snowfall for this area. But that warmth was significantly complimented by several pinnacle movements ahead in this transition.

After being released from future financial obligations after my employment separation this summer, I thought it time to pursue the formation of the foundation. I met with another attorney referred from a good friend. He is helping me struc- ture the premise and mission of the Miles in Front Foundation and is completing the paperwork for an LLC and 501(c)(3). And within our conversation, he agreed to pursue the paper- work entries for my legal name change to help smooth all other financial issues forthcoming. This will provide a basis for birth certificate and gender marker change, en route to a renewed passport and driver's license among many other sources I'll need to inform.

And after several weeks and months of dead-end searches through full-service publishers to step by step self-publishing consultants and self-help guides, I began a quest that was much more purposeful and began slowly to net some key contacts. This is greatly expedited things and put me much more directly in the driver's seat—in much better control of this book's content, distribution channels and overall preservation of ownership.

THE 'MILES IN FRONT' FOUNDATION

Seven years ago, I became firmly committed to make a difference, to establish a firm base reaching out, protecting, and advocating for the Trans community as best I could. To make a statement…to leave a legacy. To stop going through the motions waiting for something else to happen before acting on what I know. It was past time to get something done and start the next chapter of my life, the most important part of why I am still here. Looking at my past experiences including those times where I was able to escape the grip of death, I've come to realize that I was spared from those moments because of a greater purpose yet to be revealed.

Now, this begins another part of my story that is arguably the most important part of my existence. Helping rear two children was certainly a lasting legacy that I will cherish forever. But each has also another path and to date, does not include me—I suppose understandably so. I certainly hope that they will come to me one day soon.

After my mother died two years after my sister, it became clear to me I had work to do and time was growing short.

Immersing myself in the Trans community learning more about the local challenges and global violence confronting us, my mission became far more crystal. When my retirement becomes official and I am able to start this chapter, I intend to work to begin a process for which I have much to learn. That mission involves—

- Create a trust fund within the foundation to administer financial resources with a pronounced mission dedicated to the Trans community.

- Solicit sponsors to help fund the trust over many years well beyond my time here.

- Explore real estate to build or repurpose a social center where Trans persons of all ages can meet in a safe space.

- Include an attached dorm to house homeless youth and adults from the Trans community unwelcome elsewhere.

- Extend a welcoming to those also from religions of all perspectives to worship in a chapel setting where they cannot be shunned or persecuted for practicing their faith-whatever that may be—in a safe place.

- Co-matching scholarships to attend public collegiate level institutions to increase Trans opportunities in public service and political influence to help change corrupt politicians and their laws against us.

The good news? There is really no right or wrong way to do this, just my goal to leverage all that I have learned for the betterment and preservation of our Trans community as far and wide as possible. Until Trans persons are universally accepted into mainstream society and employment ranks, our mission will continue charging on. Where LGBTQ+s overall have made huge gains and inroads, there is much work left to do. There is no time like the present to get engaged and committed to stepping out and offering your talents and passion to this cause.

THE SILVER LINING

Trials and tribulations of the past and recent are not with-out their good points. Like everyone, I've had my share of each in life. There are many positive markers in my jour-ney that far outweigh the trauma. We take the bad with the good—everything is temporary. I have been blessed in many ways, among which I have tried to wise up much more in my older years sharing with others those material things and of my attention. Giving of yourself is one way to get back. I know it sounds cliché, but it's all in how you view things.

Guess I've been getting used to the day to day feeling of being sequestered during shelter in place from the Covid-19 pandemic. But it gets pretty easy to dwell on the bad things and get caught up in one's own pity party. Let's shed some light on this subject that I'm sure many can fully relate. Knowing that the societal acceptance may not achieve the degree we hope for in our lifetimes, we can only find solace in the support systems to which we ourselves extend that outreach. Let me give a few examples where my support system has expanded in places I never would have expected even during the time when my traditional means of support have left me.

You have already read where my search for a new and accepting house of worship would bring me into their family. And my quest is really to rekindle that feeling of community. I never really felt that in other places primarily because my presence wasn't well-accepted. However, my experience early this year has proved quite promising in the search of a sustainable friendship. Three extremely special ladies invited me too their GNO (girl's night out) where we celebrated each other's company—genuine smiles and presence. That made me so happy! The authenticity and honesty shown by each was priceless. Our first such meeting was last February before the Covid nightmare began full swing in a group of about 20 ladies in total. The second time was in late October where four of us donned masks sitting until late evening on an outside deck sharing stories and wine—just basking in sorely needed conversation together. Perhaps I am too easily pleased, but… I don't think so. This was a demonstration of friendship that still remains even though I only saw each of them three times last winter. Funny how first impressions work. But the lesson I learned was the need to get off my couch and extend myself to others knowing they were just as alone as I was. That honesty goes both ways.

Another key to this story has been the recent outreach some members of my original support group have returned, others remain absent. But the amazing thing is that several who were not in that original group now have shown their outreach asking for weekly Zoom meetings and personal phone calls that I had not experienced before. Quite refreshing! Seeing new faces (on Zoom) and talking person to person is a major win in my world. Most of these conversations take 30 minutes or so, some up to 90—but very welcome and anticipated.

A crucial underlying theme that perhaps you already figured out—that there is an extremely vital stage that one must reach along this path toward complete transformation and fulfillment—that of <u>liberation</u>. And I confess that I still have a long way to go, I am still a work in progress!

Maybe I refer too easily to this metaphor of a 'journey' but seems that there really is no better way to describe the process of our lifetime as a series of tests and challenges that build our character, for worse or better—or both. Within the Trans journey lies a host of such challenges that often takes baby steps to begin and a lifetime to declare that victory—or that is my definition of liberation. And from my experience, of the greatest moments in my life amidst the micro—successes, major mountains, and speed-bump challenges, none has had more profound effect on my outlook of the future than that feeling of putting those past traumas behind—essentially putting closure on these pain points. The feeling of openly professing my truth and inwardly grasping the grandeur of that pinnacle achievement is something I know I always anticipated but was so 'out there' that I never really understood it until it happened. That immense combination of internal gratitude for the happiness now experienced—coming to terms with my OWN self-worth and importance, to me, comes almost within an explosion of emotion. But to clarify, that journey is far from complete as of the date this manuscript.

To highlight those separate liberating experiences, this will recap some of those that helped my maturity and enlightenment progress more and more...

- The water and open space—Understanding the solitude and finding success within the confinements I was forced to live at the time.

- My parent's values—Questioning their choices and philosophies. 'Trying on' other experiences is a vital survival step, but also put my heart, my actions, and my motives in the right place.

- Learning by doing—From coaching & teaching, learning in the process from those whom I tutored was something I strived for, mostly because I had an immense quest for knowledge.

- On the track, in the pool, at school, and at Trans conferences—getting to know so many more who were coming from a similar spot with similar challenges!

- Stepping out—First at Rori's, out of my comfort zone into the realization it was okay to be me! Everyday are new things and encounters to 'step out' and take calculated risks.

- Getting the bigger picture—Seeing a roomful of Trans, knowing I was not sick or perverted. Understanding LGBTQ+—the breadth and diversity was SO much more!

- Announcing my boundaries—My transition is not a subject of discussion <u>unless I let it</u>.

- Removing foundations and coverups—Being able to go 'nearly naked' underneath after medical transition and hormone treatments have brought me to a place that I never thought possible. That 'freedom' was quite exhilarating. (And it cut prep time WAY down!)

- Owning my truth—face to face, the mirror tells me the truth sought for decades, I fully embrace. When I saw (and heard) that image speaking to me, I knew this was for real!

- Never apologetic for who I am—this is mine to own and I am <u>never</u> be sorry for being me.

- Not accepting those who reject me—where everyone is entitled to their own opinion, that doesn't need to affect mine nor my truth… ever again! Those days are gone, for good. I will not respect those who do not respect me or my community.

These landmarks continue to expand and are responsible for so much of my conscious liberation. Short of my children's birth, my GRS the morning after, worshiping for the first time as 'me', and my performance at the Olympic pre-trials, this ranks right up there with my purest definition of happiness. You certainly have had those in <u>your</u> journey... but never discount them, no matter how small they may seem at the time. Build on them, reflect how they impact your maturity, and never forget to count those successes. They all add up!

Part of my next chapter in life happened when I joined this wonderful group called PFLAG (Parents, Friend and Allies of Lesbians and Gays) last fall with some local leaders and organizers who have a relentless mission to pursue just as I do. They are a national support group who provides a means to reach out to families and friends of LGBTQ+s looking for answers and education to learn more about a loved one coming out or asking for any/all sources of support. Connection has been timely and quite rewarding. I've discovered that the foundation I'm planning will take root in a co-sponsorship through PFLAG and the Treehouse—an umbrella support group that will provide a physical 'safe space' and offer a means of connecting with other support missions—even around the country if needed. When I was asked to be on the Treehouse board, I jumped for joy (as high as I am able given my age and physically challenged jumping at all). We hope that this will be the perfect springboard for The Miles in Front Foundation whose mission is to establish a safe place for homeless Trans and to meet, socialized, and convene in meaningful discussions for support systems where questions of conflict are constant issues.

LIFE'S BALANCE SHEET

Everyone goes through life experiences with those pinnacle moments to cherish and look back on as something wonderful and enlightening during a given moment in time. But we also enter this world with no guarantees of rich blessings of any kind or quantity. Some may even start this life with disease or handicaps that further demonstrate how unfair and varied those situations can be from the first breath until the last.

Where my messages are not to demonstrate the definition or validation of privilege, however, are merely intended to offer one perspective how life balance sheet sometimes it is clearly off-balance. Even in my younger years I recall relationships with situations of pain, frustration, and anger that challenged me with finding the useful lessons and blessings even in the hardest times. In my youth, I seemed to discover a way too intentionally bury that pain and remove some of the deepest hurt from my memory. If I were to try to recall many of my attempted relationships in my adolescent years, many of those are buried in forgotten memories mostly because of the pain they were causing and my choice to distance myself from those. Where it tends to work in the short-term, it tends also

to mask my underlying insecurities. It might fulfill the immediate discomfort I had experienced, but it also can increase
one's numbness to other similar situations. It was not until
my later years when I discovered how to deal with that kind of
pain and asked for renewal, understanding and forgiveness. In
my world, one more way that God has saved me from myself.

Have you ever described someone as 'difficult to love'? I
know I probably fit that category with many relationships.
Using the concept of the balance sheet also gives credibility
to that [once again] analogy of the 'train-ride of life'. Working
through life as a train ride in which people and acquaintances
on both sides of the balance sheet get on an off that train at
various points in one's life. My life's experience has demonstrated that there are fewer long-term riders on my train but
of a quality that only comes a source far greater than me. These
are people of which some are discussed in previous chapters
in this book, however, does not representing everyone on my
journey.

Use every moment you can to plant seeds for those new
'riders' on that train and to nurture the ones you cherish and
hope to grow alongside your travels. I acknowledge in full
transparency that I did not take my own counsel very well
most of which waited way too long before I gave this any
attention or credibility. Where I am a work in progress, I do
believe that I have made some valuable strides and discovered
in my later years how important it is that I make up for lost
time NOW. To those who have been steadfast on my 'Black'
side of the balance sheet and even those on the 'Red' side, you
have taught me much and gone to great lengths to form who

I have become. Thank you!

Now for the best moments in my next chapter of life… this is THE real reason I exist and am on this Earth. And why I've been spared from myself so many times, demonstrating the patience and love only He has. This Foundation will happen, and it will be a testament to both my faith and my resolve to help bring the Trans community into mainstream society, none of whom should ever have to 'hide in plain sight'.

(Endnotes)

1   Human Rights Campaign (HRC); 'Violence Against the Transgender Community in 2019'

2   HRC Foundation 2018 report on 'Dismantling a Culture of Violence'

TAKING CARE OF YOU!

Making note of all the twists and turns in this journey, my story really is not much different from yours. But with all the constant demands on my responsibilities all these years, the one part consistently neglected most every time was me. Where I am certain I have come up short many times, foremost in my mind was ALWAYS how my actions and follow-through on commitments to others took center stage for most of that lifetime. Perhaps, one can argue, it was simply my lack of courage to confront the truth I have always known was mine to recapture and reveal. Maybe that's true. But whatever your age, background, culture, or support system, every step is YOUR choice dependent solely on YOUR circumstances. My delay was purposeful in most situations as these pages meticulously demonstrate—not offered as excuses, rather helps to paint a picture of reality that under the circumstances, offered few other options—most times none at all. Those early days were extremely dangerous treading on uncharted ground that bordered on a death sentence in some circles.

But I do not intend to make comparisons to other's situations—everyone is unique with different conditions and variables. Yours may be similar in some ways, but likely altogether different in many others. For most, your outreach to a strong and loving support system has had or can have immeasurable value. I did not have that until only a few years ago, and much of that has come and gone and come again. That train keeps moving and passengers keep boarding, some stay put for the entire trip, others for a very short—but important time spent with you.

It's extremely important to call attention to one major underlying theme in this story. This has been a life-long struggle separating personal pain from critical life lessons all with a climax ending with forgiveness—of other's actions or omissions, and of my own misgivings and distrust. Reconciling actions is a perpetual challenge that, unless one makes that diligent effort time after time, will consume your world, and take you with it if you let it. Without closure and forgiveness, progress will <u>never</u> happen, and love will <u>never</u> materialize. Where no one with values and a conscience can dispute the pain you've endured from similar experiences and outright shuning or denial, it's critical that each of us learn from those experiences and put them behind us. Not to forget, but to learn through forgiveness. This is among the best way to take care of YOU.

Although there were several times in these pages where my experiences demanded some 'self-preserving' decisions, there comes a point where your struggle for doing what you know to be right takes on another critical factor—YOU! Conducting day to day assignments and fulfillment of other's expectations often may have little direct consideration of how you fit into this equation—especially if you have not had that conversation with those setting those expectations.

As the Covid-19 outbreak has taught many, ignoring yourself in these exceedingly difficult times has ramifications. Getting caught up in the frenzy of all the surrounding expectations of keeping us all protected, still caring for family and loved ones, often puts your interests last. Just ask the frontline healthcare professionals who are those who put themselves at risk every day they put others health before their own. Where the comparison is not exact, it does demonstrate the deep seated mental (and physical) health of those who put other's needs and expectations often neglect their own. And over time can lead to critical damage where a reliable support system can be a Godsend.

You are the best judge of who you can approach when to tell them what you are wrestling with. In the absence of supportive family or friends, never give up hope! These days, I would have traded my entire swimming 'career' to have the outreach and loving support of LGBTQ+ agencies. At least my questions could have been answered and my search for a stronger connection would not have been so delayed.

In short, give yourself a break! Yes, this is a journey about and for YOU. Spending all that time accommodating others tends to put YOU on that back burner leaving little choice for your future until YOU decide enough is enough.

HOW DO YOU DEFINE LOVE?

Probably the million-dollar question that will net that many answers for most people. Most can probably define a handful, others perhaps only one, yet still others an infinite number of types and sources. Your specific definition will be subject to life experiences and to whom you received and gave your love in various circumstances and relationships.

From my years, my most rewarding, meaningful, and lasting relationships have started out in a vastly different way from the way they have progressed. I suppose the best way I approach this abstract concept is not as much 'how' I love, but who and why. For instance, I love…

My Children—Above all the rest, you are my legacy and from whom most of my tears, fears, and jubilation is sourced. From the moment a parent helps to birth their children, they are forever changed. Each of you will forever love differently and more selflessly—you just will!

After coming out to my son I remember his slight pause giving me ample time to read his mind. My quick reaction followed—*"I will never regret having you as my children. You are my pride and my legacy. You are very often the reasons I do what I do the way I do. Don't think for a minute that I do not cherish each of you constantly."*

My Best Friends—I can probably count on two hands those who are deserving of that label in my world (Donna, Kathy, Dan, Christina, Paul, Lisa, Barb, Elizabeth, Laura, Rori, to name a few). But that's also how I roll—quality, not quantity. There are some who have lasted decades and others who have stepped off the train of life and on the same tracks I'm on. Neither makes one more important than the other, only to demonstrate the truth in that analogy. But THE key distinction of friendship is that which has withstood the intricate details of my transition and loved me because of it, not in spite of it. Simply put, without that continuation of friendship after being informed of my truth, gives me the indication the friendship had a shallow foundation in the first place. Those who have earned my BFF designation (and you know who you are) have earned their place on my 'honor roll' purely from being who they are. No effort, just by being themselves! THAT is gift enough.

My Faith—This is the point to which I firmly reinforce my love and commitment to the one who owns my soul. I've never questioned that and contrary to some religious authorities, I have no need to reaffirm that commitment. It's never been stronger and never been questioned. Yes, I have had my arguments, but I've lost everyone. I openly admit I'm a work in progress even at this advanced age. But I also have pride and love for what He has done in my life and the person He has revealed before my eyes, has always been 'right in front of me'. Amidst my struggles and tears, I have never questioned

His place in my life. I have completely surrendered!

<u>My Family</u>—From my childhood to current day, those relationships have changed considerably. No longer are my parents or middle sister living, and the remaining siblings do not know me—nor do I suspect they ever will. My arms and heart will open immediately upon request, but I don't anticipate that ever happening. The tears I've shed for them have subsided—the pain and hurt induced by ignoring me or my reality shared has taken its toll. But I still understand and cherish each my brother and older sister—they are my family, and I would come to their aid if I were summoned or needed. My only condition? That I am who I am—always! Those days of hiding in plain sight are done. And to no one I apologize, except the simple reality that I concealed that truth for <u>far too long</u>.

<u>My Partner</u>—At the moment, a placeholder only. Where there is no current occupant, someday there shall be. And with past relationships, I am a strong and devoted partner with immense conviction and abounding love. But also demanding of respect and offering space. Where a partnership is to join as one is not to suggest removing the individual qualities that make up those people. In actuality, I've found that the stronger relationships allow those unique traits to surface and flourish growing and serving as examples to each other. I know of no other formula for success. Love is love! And in my relation-ships, I offer a deep friendship as a foundational characteristic that has no limits or constraints. A love that sees through the transparency of my skin and loves me for who I am, and I love her for who she is—that defines the love of my life.

Agape Love—the bond of caring with deep respect for others who share my belief systems, often what I refer to as my 'church community'. Some may define this in their world, as a 'Christian' love, but I take a slightly different approach. I am not here to sell or promote any religion, only to demonstrate the difference and influence that I believe such a spiritual guide helps me through this life and all the trials that come with it—by my definition, my God, or my Christ. To each their own how they choose to lead their life or even if there is or is not such a guiding force in your life. All I can do is show you the times and situation He has brought me through in complete victory, but in His time—NOT mine.

My Deacon —assigned to me before surgery was a gift from God sending me an Angel. Anne was one of the most beautiful people I have ever been blessed to meet-no exaggeration, simply fact. She was, to me, what I suppose I can best describe as my definition of 'Christ with skin on'. She opened her arms to me shortly after I first appeared on the scene within months after I had moved here. She and her new bride had made this a home also and their youth, enthusiasm and selfless giving were clear indications of their genuine love of their God and their community. She openly brought me into their world and welcomed me in more ways than this book has pages. In the spring of 2016 when I had made my decision to proceed with GRS, she quickly and decisively volunteered to provide me one-way transportation to Philadelphia that upcoming fall. And to seal the deal— an act above all acts—she volunteered to act as a caregiver overseeing my recovery during that first week in rehab. Who does that? The quick and easy answer—Anne does! And for no other reason than love. She had said several times before that week, *"I want to be there before you go into surgery and be the first thing you see when you come out to recovery."* In my previous six decades of life, never has there been a better more shining example of Agape love. Thank you for sharing your selfless love!

<u>My Companions</u>—Coming in many shapes and sizes, breeds and species, I've had my share of felines, canines and even a few fish—yes, all of whom I can say I loved dearly. After discovering in 2007 I was allergic to most felines, unfortunately that cut out many potential roommates. Fritz was a beautiful long-haired black cat with a white bow tie looked like the perfect formalwear on four legs. He was not my first choice in the room at the Humane Center, but I was drawn to him and he to me. The next three years were packed with joy surrounding his playfulness with me. My house had an L-shaped stairwell landing that became marked overtime with a black smudge on the wall where he would throw himself after playfully chasing me in the dark. I would feel a series of repeated paddles around my lower legs where he was trying to climb up and play. Previous owners had him declawed earlier which rendered him defenseless outside. And that playfulness contributed to his demise when one day he escaped the protective confinement of my house never to be seen again. I'm certain he would not have made it through the evening. This was my first encounter with such immense sadness for an animal that became a major part of me. Not long after I had received the results from an annual physical exam that

confirmed my fears of allergic reaction to some animals—most specifically from animal dander and unkept long hair. Fritz was very well groomed—so much so that he won 'best in show' in a local expo, mostly from his performance as the only one playful enough to grab onto the dangling toy in a way he used to hug and paddle my legs. Beautiful!

My next major love affair was with my four Ladies—one Pekinese and three Shih Tzu sisters (same father, two mothers). Quite the challenge taking our daily walks with four separate leashes in the winter. Wearing a glove on each hand and sep-arating each doing their business required significant patience and devotion to their cause. But it was time well spent! They were THE only source of requited love during most of my adult 'discovery' time of this journey. Their constant presence, persistent interest, and intelligence were remarkable traits akin to most humans. They experienced their own emotions and took on the demeanor of my mood or condition at the time. Never in my life have I experienced the devotion and uncondi-tional love they truly exemplify. Each of them is sorely missed, often THE source of my tears in a wave of despair comes over me. I look forward to a search for a new companion that will begin shortly, but my challenge is to avoid limiting that search to those new companions who may not compare with these Ladies.

My Pastor—Where I have had several throughout my faith and transition journey, each has had a significant impact on me in more than one way. One in particular certainly stands apart from the rest in an easily discernable way— Pastor Barb. For me, she was there at the *"Right time and right place*", but I should add that she also had the "R*ight message, the right way.*"

Barb was an integral role acting as a coach and increasing my trust factor significantly. That sense of community and reaching out to the Trans persons was a risk she willingly accepted challenging herself and her congregation to embrace their own mission. She was witness to her own growth over her short assignment—an extremely difficult post everyone knew full well (a caveat with her pastoral contract) when her term concluded that there would be an equal end to all of those relationships she had built, leaving the permanent pastor, when installed, tasked with determining a plan about how to continue. Where that may have been slightly less painful for church members losing only one relationship, Barb had invested her heart and soul into a congregation full of very real personal commitments—all within her attempt to limit the extent of emotional involvement she could be losing in spite. To illustrate her growth over our short time together, the vastness of her unselfish gift of love can best be demonstrated by her own testimony following a read of this manuscript—

> *Teri —I am not sure how to best say "thank you" for the privilege of reading your manuscript. You have so much courage and determination to put your life into print. Thank you for doing this —your words will provide love for those who choose to read it in the spirit of growth. I continue to have deep gratitude that our paths crossed and that you chose to offer me gracious love as I stumbled through learning and becoming more aware. You were compassionate and gentle with my ignorance and provided me opportunity*

after opportunity to grow. I had so many thoughts and emotions as I read your story that I am not sure where to begin.

I knew there would be painful parts to your story but knowing that logically didn't truly prepare me for the profound vulnerability you undertook in choosing to share your journey for others to read. I have no words to express how I felt as you named and recognized the pain you have experienced throughout your life —from your dad's inability to affirm and love who you are to your daughter's inability to live out the words you were once offered. It is my prayer that in sharing this, you might somehow reduce the pain that others face since you were also able to share an integrated view of how your pain has impacted the strength in you today —two sides to the same coin in a way, one side pain and the other side strength/love. I hate that you (and so many others) had to walk down a road where you could not experience the joy of being who you were created to be, and I grieve that our world extracts that from so many. I am so grateful that you have stayed strong in your faith and that you are so intentional about your spirituality. Thank you for being a shining example of keeping your relationship with God above the fray of this world.

Over the last 3-4 years, I have met a number of folks who are not ready to come out in public life as the costs for a person in the Trans community is so incredibly dangerously high. Too many have not had the experiences you had of looking in the mirror to feel authenticity, joy, and pride. I know it is getting better—baby steps —but it is still not nearly enough. Thank you for your commitment to change this and to provide opportunity and support for those who need it.

I hope that with time, I can grow into a better ally. I still have much to learn and I ask for your forgiveness that I wasn't able to offer you more as your pastor —but you caught me at the beginning of the learning curve (and Lord do I have a long way to go).

God created such a bright light in you, and it is wonderful to see it shine. Please know that I have the highest respect and admiration for you and for your contributions in life. You are living out your calling and I thank God for that —there are many people who never have the full courage to do what they are called/ created to do.

Again, thank you for the privilege of reading your memoir. Reading it only increased my respect and admiration for you.

Peace,

Barb

Barb's character and love was equally matched by her humility and authenticity. What you saw is exactly what you got. She will forever be one of <u>my</u> greatest definitions of 'love in Christ'.

<u>My Community</u>—My love for each of you is undeniable and indisputable. Eight years ago, my move here was with the intent to fulfill a mission to educate, protect, finance where possible, and devote time and energies to/for the transgender community. That mission has only grown in intensity and importance to me—something I intend to drive forward. But for now, I have to pull out the stops and demonstrate my love for you in every way I can, beginning today with this message

and the 'Miles in Front Foundation' that is established to continue this mission long after I am gone. Know that you are loved deeply and constantly! There are many other sources and examples of loving relationships in my life and in yours. I invite readers to take a moment devoted to appreciating life's blessings no matter how obscure or insignificant they may seem they are very real and likely more important than you think.

A final message here? It seems there is no loss of anger and banter on social media and daily interaction these days. And with suicide prevention agencies experiencing daily interventions with those feeling outcast or denied this foundational need (arguably second only to basic physical needs), maybe it's time in your life to call attention to those you love—perhaps whom you have not told in a while.

LOVE IS LOVE! CHERISH IT, PLANT IT, NOURISH IT!

EPILOGUE

What if... everyone alive was blind? From age 10 to 50... we could see at birth, to learn and to grow. But beginning our second decade of life our sight was taken from us as a message of love without judgment... without cause or denial of truth... and then restored when/if we reached our 50th birthday? That for the simple purpose of helping teach those without sight that judgment has no place on this planet—that respect and love are the ONLY acceptable behaviors and values.... What if...?

Much like John Lennon's dream of *"Imagine"* a world without war, one is often left with wondering what this world would be like if we lost our sight in arguably the most important years of our lives? I can only relate from my personal experience that I never understood the concept of prejudice, separatism, or even slavery, for that matter, until my collegiate years. Part of that was from my narrow-minded parental perspective translated with how they brought up their children. But it was also a clear isolation of both my social relations with others in my childhood and that lack of much direct content in school curriculum or from those who 'taught' me. My first sociology class was a required course in college where the concepts were first introduced to me—during the final years of the Vietnam War that was driving the SDS (students for democratic society) marches on campus that screamed to me to get more involved and educated. I learned quickly that I was NOT of the same cloth as my parents, not just different in gender, but in values, mores, and my innate ability to love unconditionally. Where did that come from? Simply... from my God.

Without sight, judgment of others has a distinct disadvantage. Fundamentally, as the social species we are, we tend to fixate on those things we can only grasp through our visual perception. How can our hearts see what our eyes cannot? In a world where that judgment is handicapped, how would Native Americans, Blacks, Latinos, Jews, Arabs, Muslims, Indians, disabled persons, etc., ... and LGBTQ+s be all accepted, just the same as anyone or everyone?...What if that was more than acceptance, but embracing and engaging? ... What if?

Writing is power! But that isn't why I chose to do this— early on I mentioned that this was a critical exercise in therapy—being able to clear my mind to put those things festering where they belong... in the past, but to learn and grow from them all. Putting closure on countless pain points has served its purpose well!

This story of my life is only one perspective. Everyone is different and no one is spared constant obstacles or is blessed only with smooth sailing all the time. It takes a lifetime of choices, relentless challenges, and the faith—in my world— that I have found immensely valuable. Again, I am not selling

any reader on any religion or sect at all—just demonstrating
His value in my life and where I feel that I would be without
Him. Where that has been tested daily, I return to Him each
time with a greater sense of understanding and joy. Where I
am often by myself, I am never alone. Some may say I'm misguided or maybe even crazy, perhaps that is an element in all of
us. But I do know the times I've been rescued and those where
prayers have been answered, I choose to continue to believe
this way. It makes me whole!

My gender and my sexuality have <u>never</u> been in question,
not to me nor to my God. And that's really all that matters.
And when that time comes, my death can never touch my
truth. I am just sorry I lied to so many people [and to myself]
for so long. I didn't feel there was another choice. But hiding is
no longer a battle I need to fight—because I have won, finally!

I am not naive enough to think I won't be challenged by
those who take exception with my choices. But these were
never choices. I will stand tall with any and all of the Trans
community and will support all of you as you continue your
fight to be respected and loved because of your identity, not in
spite of it.

Most Sunday mornings on my way to church, I often pass
an intersection where the cross streets convene with one named
after an 18th century US president and the other after my 'first'
birth name given by my parents. I often smile when I pass this
only because it serves to remind me of one of the primary parts
of my past—much of which served me well in getting to where
I am now. I realize that this flies in the face of many Trans M
to F transitions, having heard so many stories of those who

'hate' their male selves. With possibly the rare exception of historic narcissistic self-professed leaders, I have very little capacity to hate anyone—let alone someone who occupied my being for six decades. I am NOT two different people—I am the same inside I have always been and was borne as—it is only my true gender that I have withheld for this time. So why would I ever hate that same person before as now? Just a fundamental premise, to me.

Many LGBTQ's will struggle with gender identity their entire lifetime, as was my journey in this story. And mine is not done yet. There were times in the early 2000s where I insisted that I was bi-gender, a more androgynous identity that allowed me the fluidity between hiding at work and presenting as myself most everywhere else. But I soon discovered, admitting to myself that this identity could not be hidden anymore for anyone's convenience or expectation. It was mine to own. And mine to change! There are also those who take exception with how long it took me to come out and some who felt I was not being true to myself because of that delay. For this, I offer some suggestions to those contemplating a monumental move to truth—

- This is your life—no one else's. Where that can sound like martyrdom, no one can deny its truth. Nor yours.

- You choose when the time is right. You will know if you listen to your heart. Where is strong support system certainly helps, they don't know all the details surrounding the nuances of your struggle and circumstances.

- Take calculated risks where they make sense to you. Not everyone is as anal as I am, but it generally serves me well. ALWAYS be safe when questions surface... take care of YOU!

- Exercise your faith where it means something to you. He is there for you If you ask Him.

- Surround yourself with a support system that understands your challenge and demonstrates strong advocacy. Where that may sound like a difficult task, and in some cases certainly is, there are numerous support agencies that will extend loving help and guidance for you. No longer do you need to suffer or be alone.

- Love and support take many different forms, and 'family' does too. Allies need to be sure you are showing up and being authentic for those you support—there are so many counting on your love!

- Parents often define their role as doing what they think is best for their children. But above all, their job is to love them for who they are and where they are.

- Extend that love and respect to yourself. No matter where you are on the identity continuum, don't shove yourself in a 'box' just because everyone else is trying to find a classification for you.

To reflect for a moment on the book introduction, my love for those who care to join me on this journey and the bond we share supporting each other is what gives me strength and gets me through many days. This crazy thing we were all born into called life never came with instructions and the human 'race' is never won. But know that among the greatest gifts you've been given are hope, love, and the grace of our God. Again, none of this is to sell you on religion, rather to restate how powerful He has been in my life. And I will take that to my grave.

My belief system is probably pretty unique—at least this is how I choose to view my origin. Of fundamental importance is that I believe my spirit chose this particular body at birth—I am a firm believer that our spirit or soul each has a bi-gendered role that isn't decided until well after the body is chosen by that spirit. Prescribing a lifelong sentence by looking at one's genitalia at birth does not fulfill this tenant—to me. My God gave me that choice but also granted me His decision to the time [when] of that birth and duration [how long] of that life—the beginning and the end. Because that choice of where and of whom my spirit would occupy was my choosing, God did not make a mistake. He made me who I am from birth and knew me only as Teri from that moment on. It was I who confused matters by choosing a body that had to be adjusted later in life. As I did. That was among the challenges God has helped me through in His time. That is my cross to bear.

It would be easy to throw my early years of childhood down the drain, knowing now what I do and looking back wondering why I failed to respond a certain way or pursue a different path early on the way I did. But we are all cast in a world without consciously choosing that purpose—at least that is how I see it in my life. Where my spiritual beliefs differ from most, among the most profound would be my origin and how that relates to my change later in life. This is a fundamental tenant of how I view my origin, my path, and my relationship. Thank you, my God, for speaking to me, for always being visible and showing me your direction giving me the wisdom to listen and act.

Use this book to serve YOU as one more beacon of hope.

NEVER GIVE UP!
NEVER STOP LOVING!

Mom at Age 20

Paul Revere for Halloween

The Quad

Skiing in the Upper Midwest

Adult Halloween

Dinner and Dancing

Conference Attendee 2009

Conference Speaker 2010

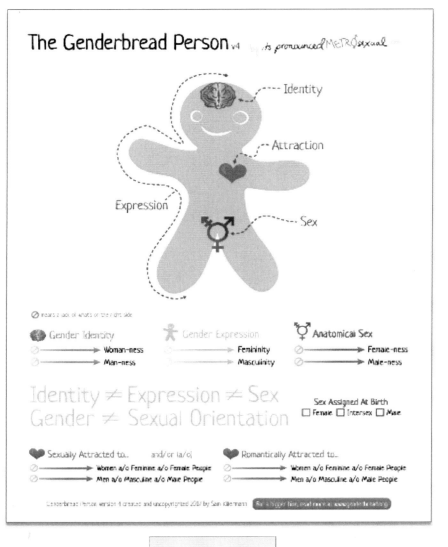

The 'Genderbread Person'

Day Tour Kayak

Training for 2009 Senior Games

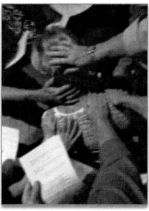

Laying On of the Hands

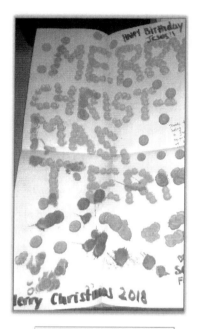

Next Door Neighbor Kids Gift

Post-Surgery Gift

Expo for June Pride Week

Dinning Out with a Friend

Story Telling for Church
During June Pride Week

'Sammie' on Ice

TDoR 2020

Sadie Saying Goodbye

Kathy & Dennis

Martin's Gift

The Advocacy 'Path' (5 A's)

- **Aversion** (distrust or dislike)
- **Ambivalence** (simultaneous conflicting reactions, beliefs, or feelings)
- **Acceptance** (recognizing a process or condition (often a negative or uncomfortable situation) without attempting to change it or protest it
- **Alliance** (joined together for mutual benefit or some common purpose)
- **Advocacy** (aims to influence decisions within political, economic, and social systems such as public policy, laws and budgets by using facts, their relationships, the media, and messaging to educate government officials and the public)

The 5 A's of Advocacy

My Four Companions

© Reprinted with permission from Alison Peacock Photography

Formal Dance
2009